MYSTIC FOREST of CHI

&

FASHION VICTIM STREET

- - -

COLORING BOOK

2 BOOK BUNDLE

MYSTIC FOREST of CHI

Coloring Book For Adults

Fantasy Art Coloring Book For Stress Relief

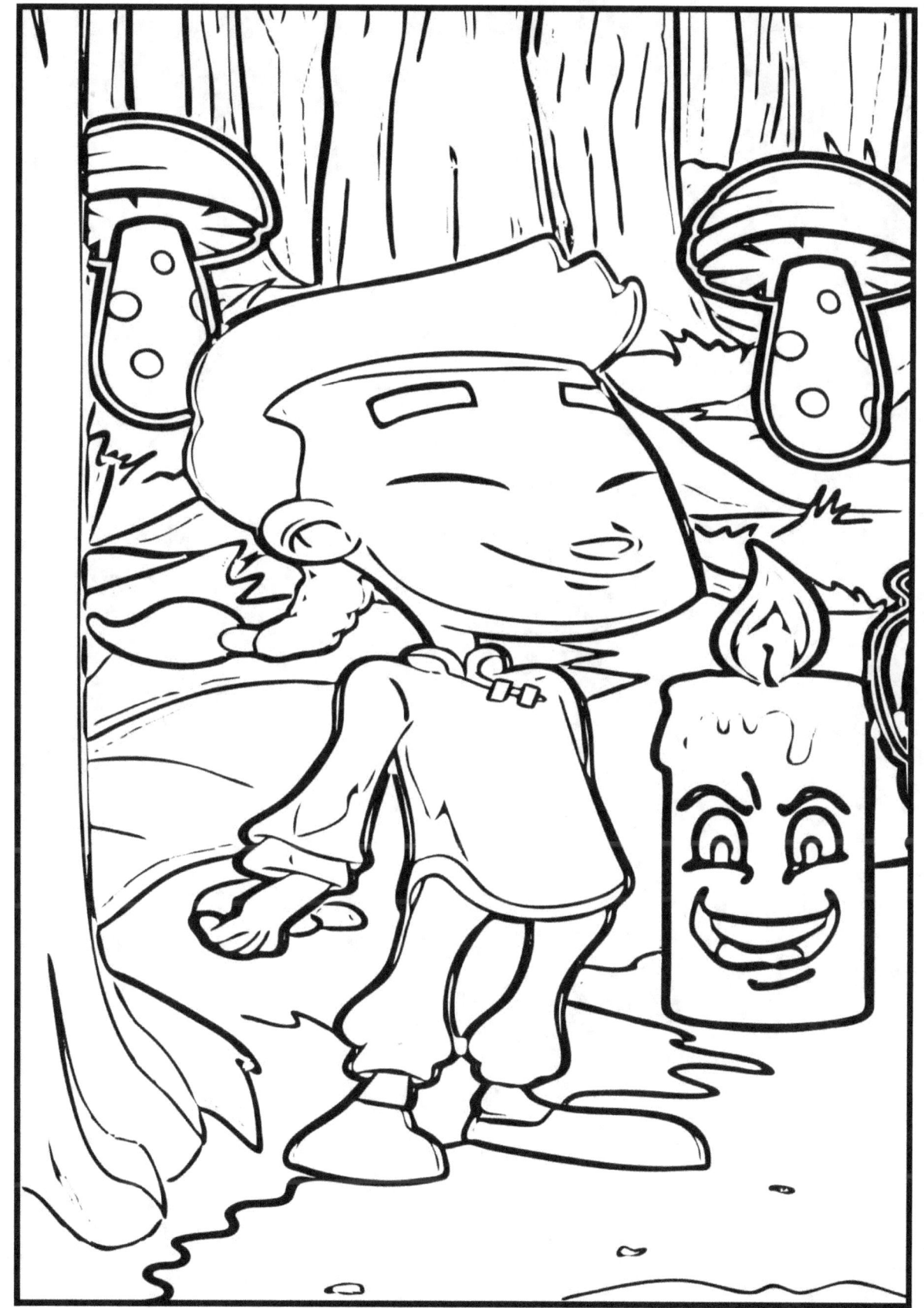

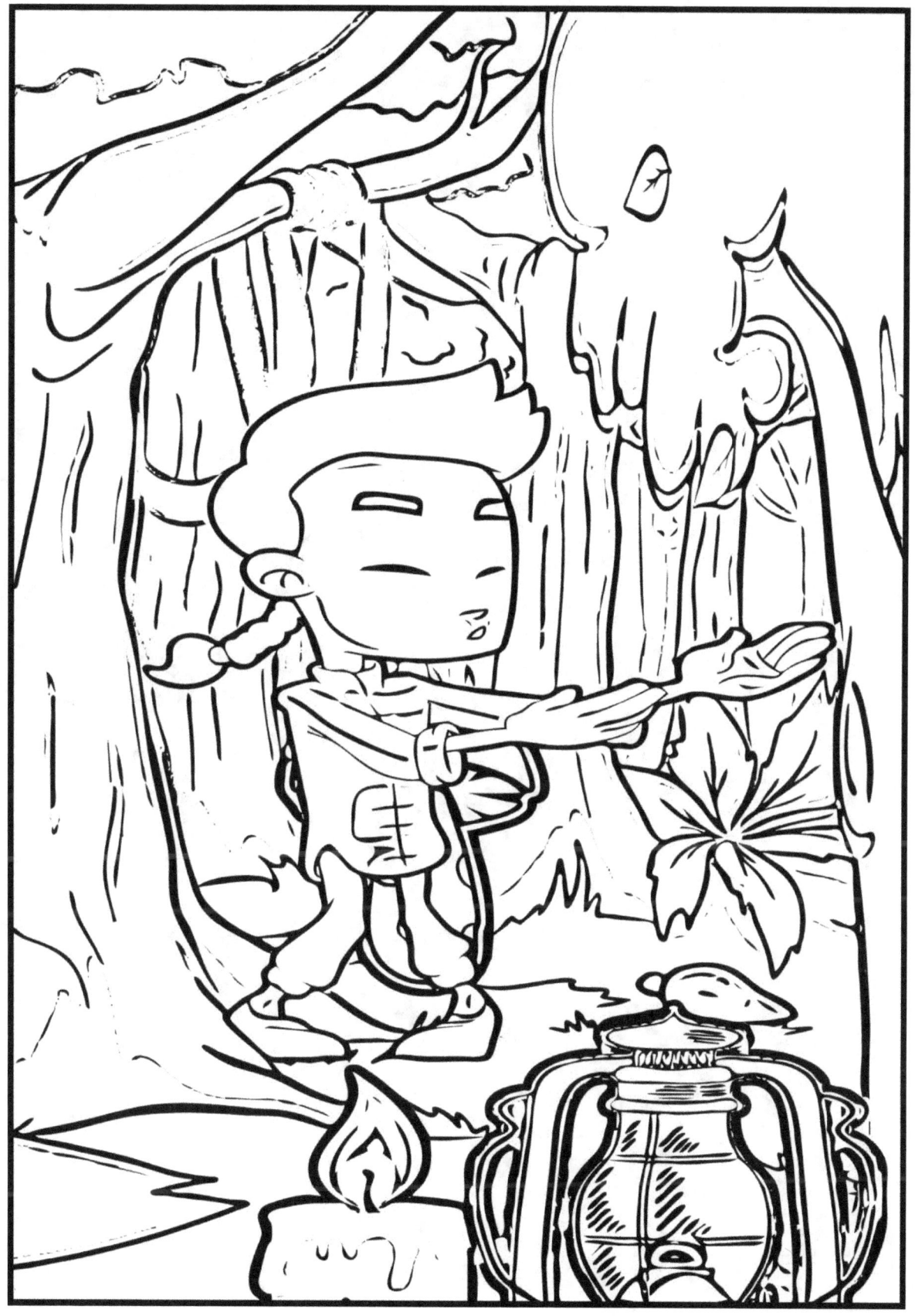

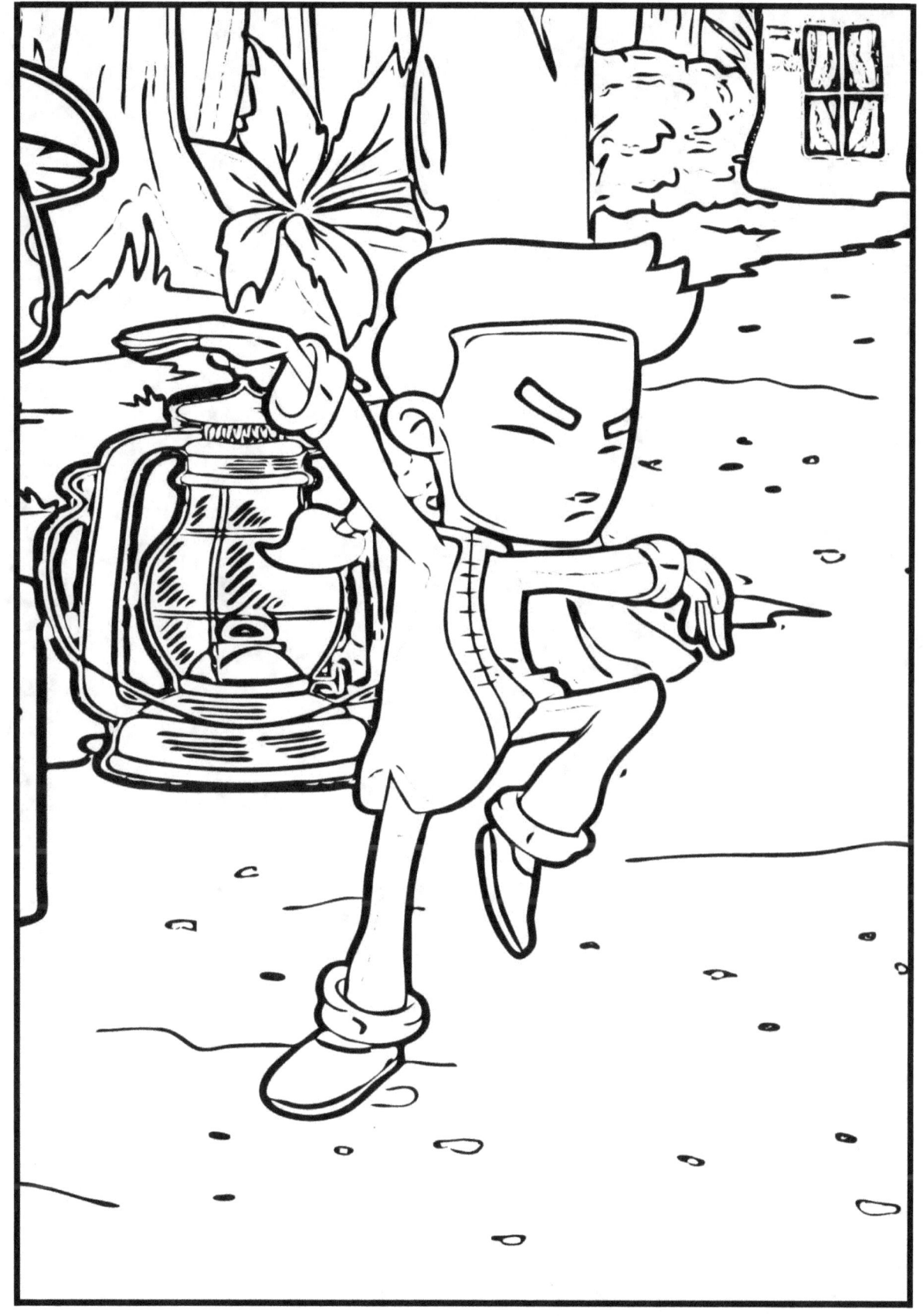

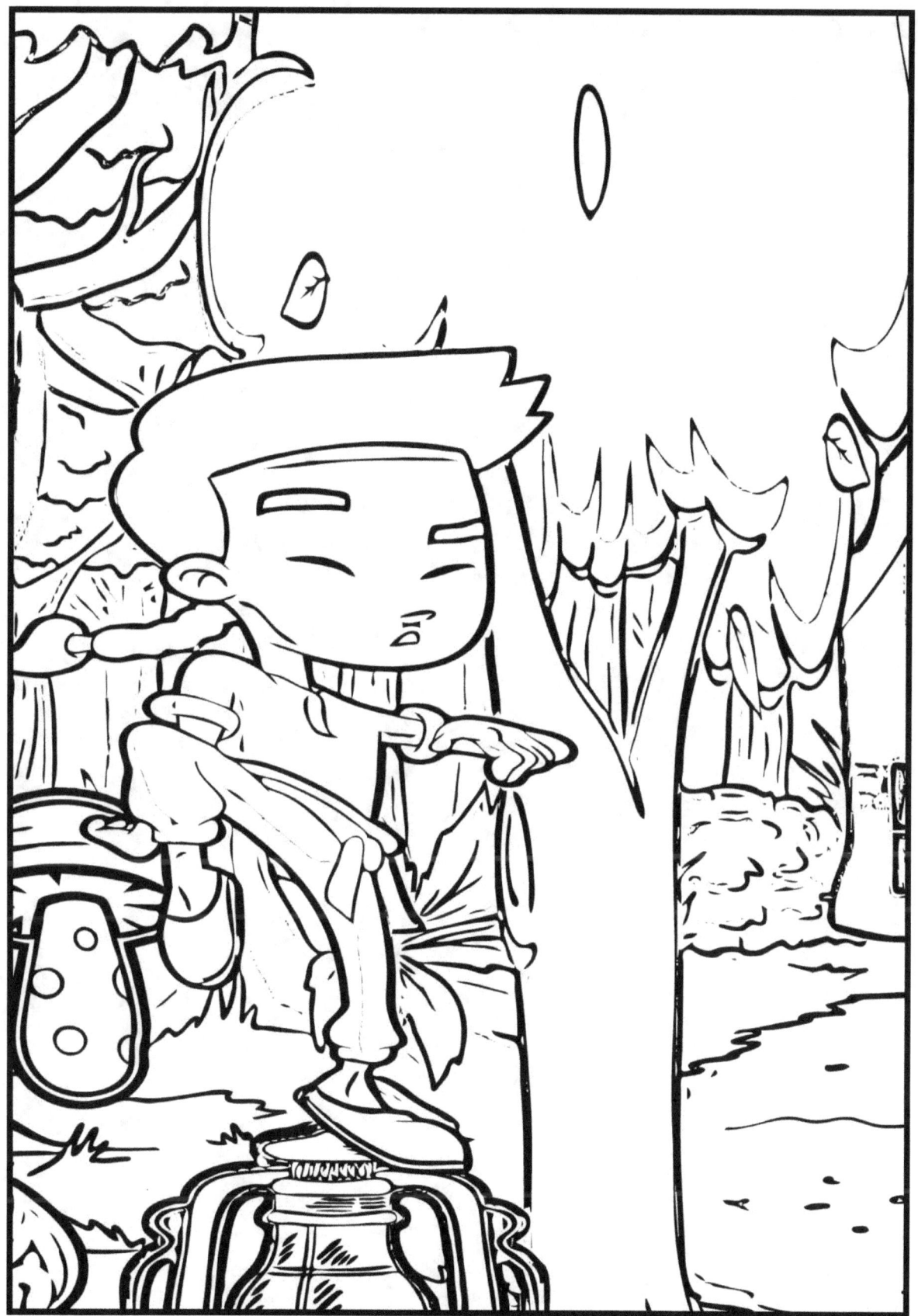

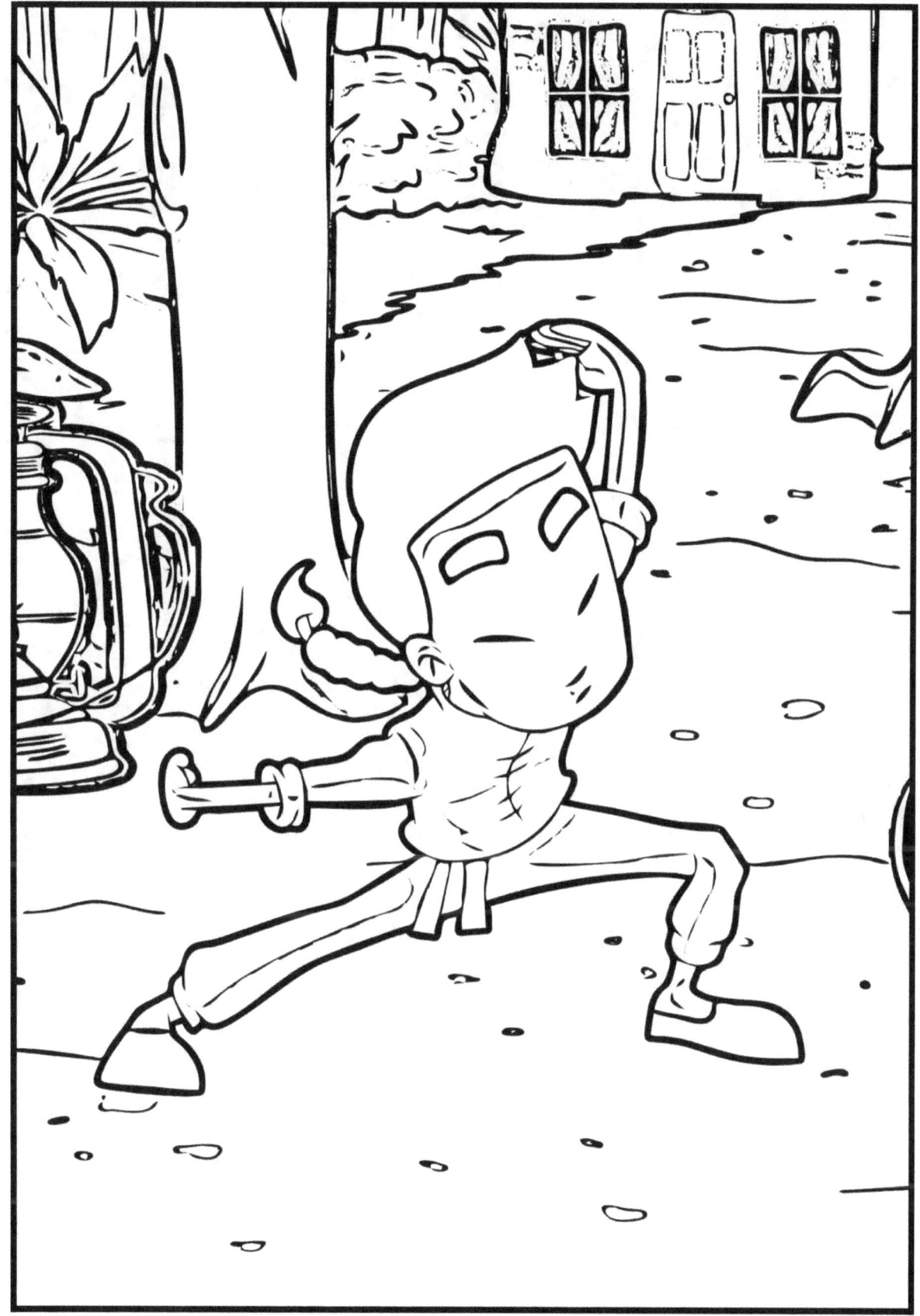

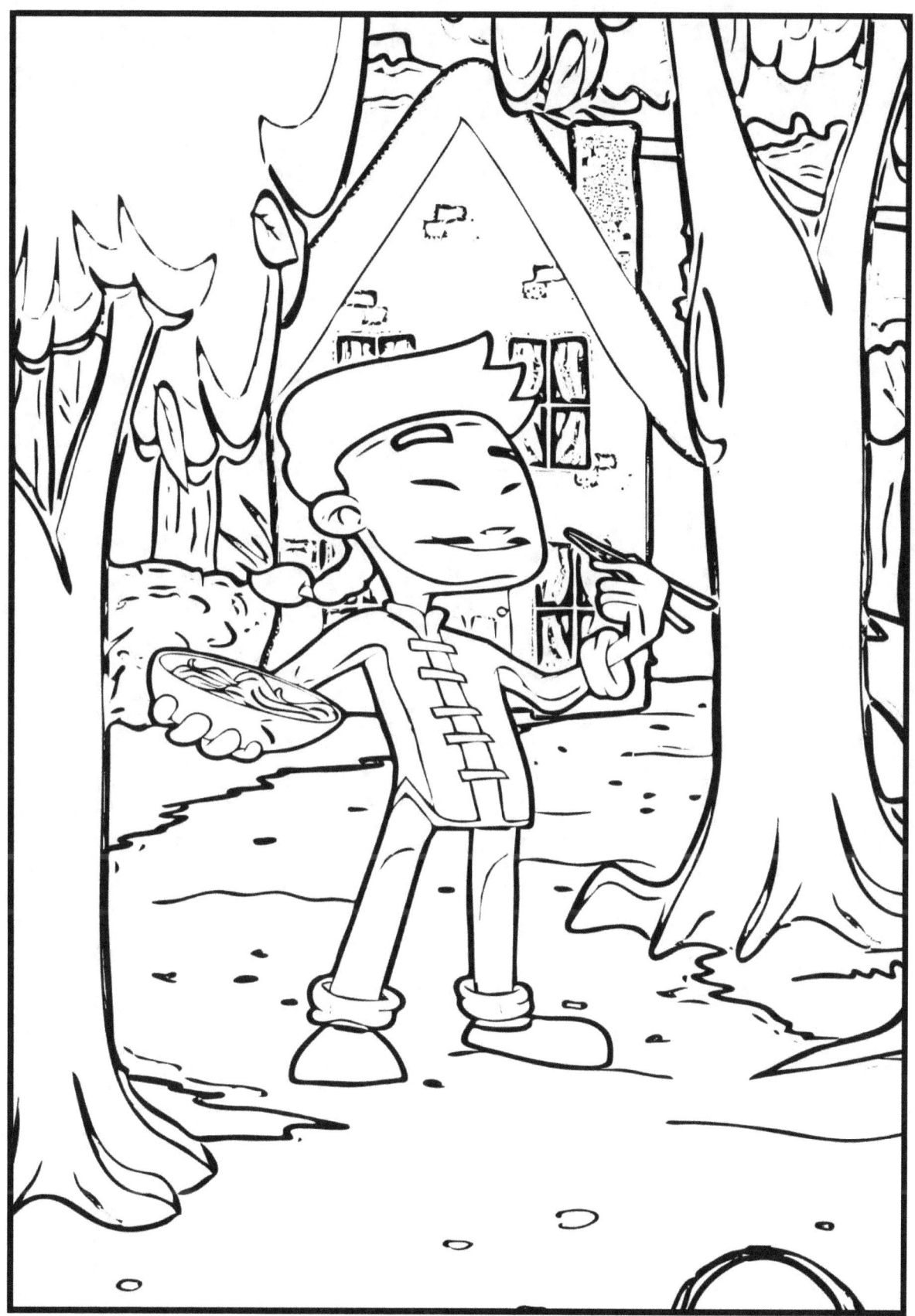

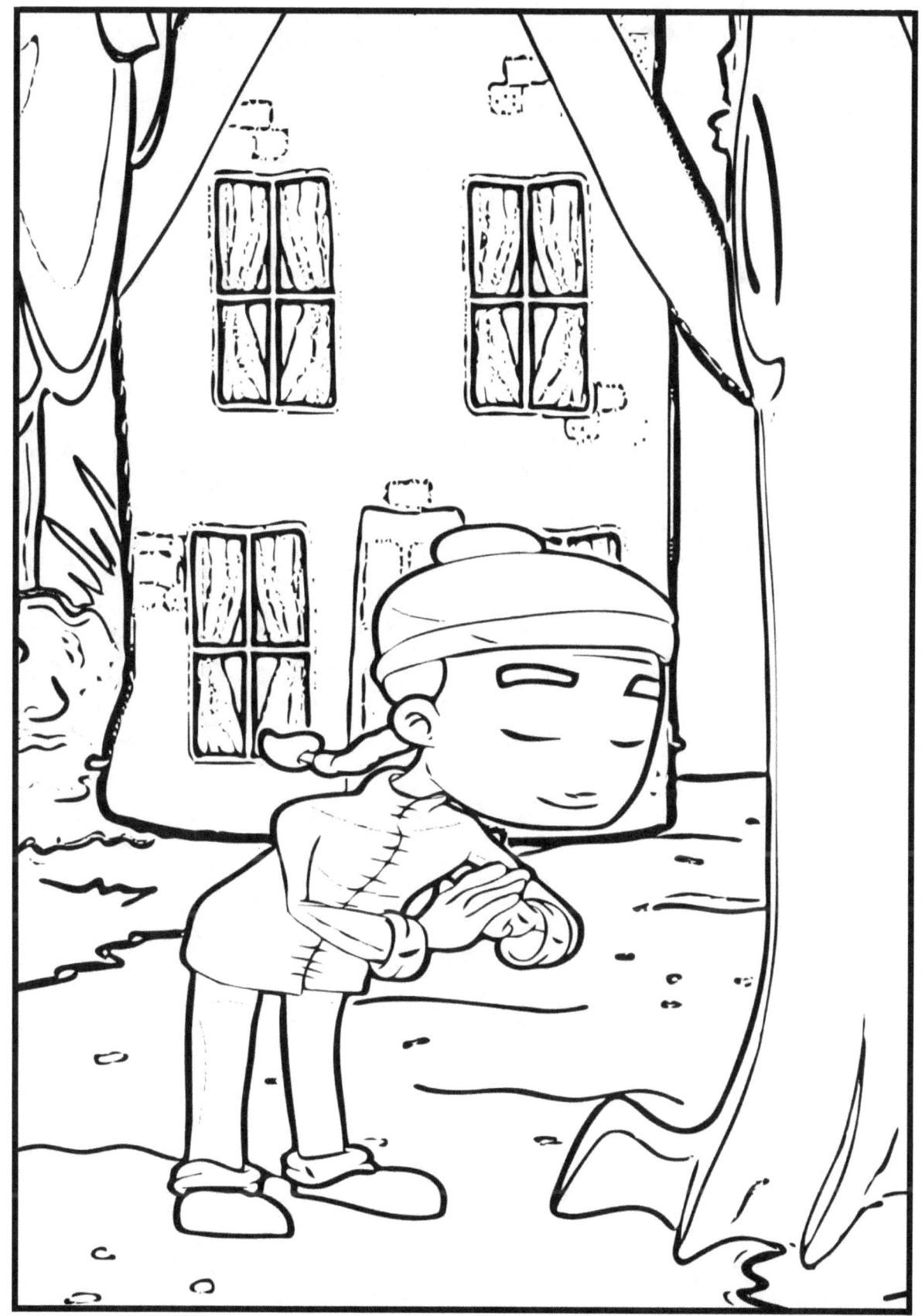

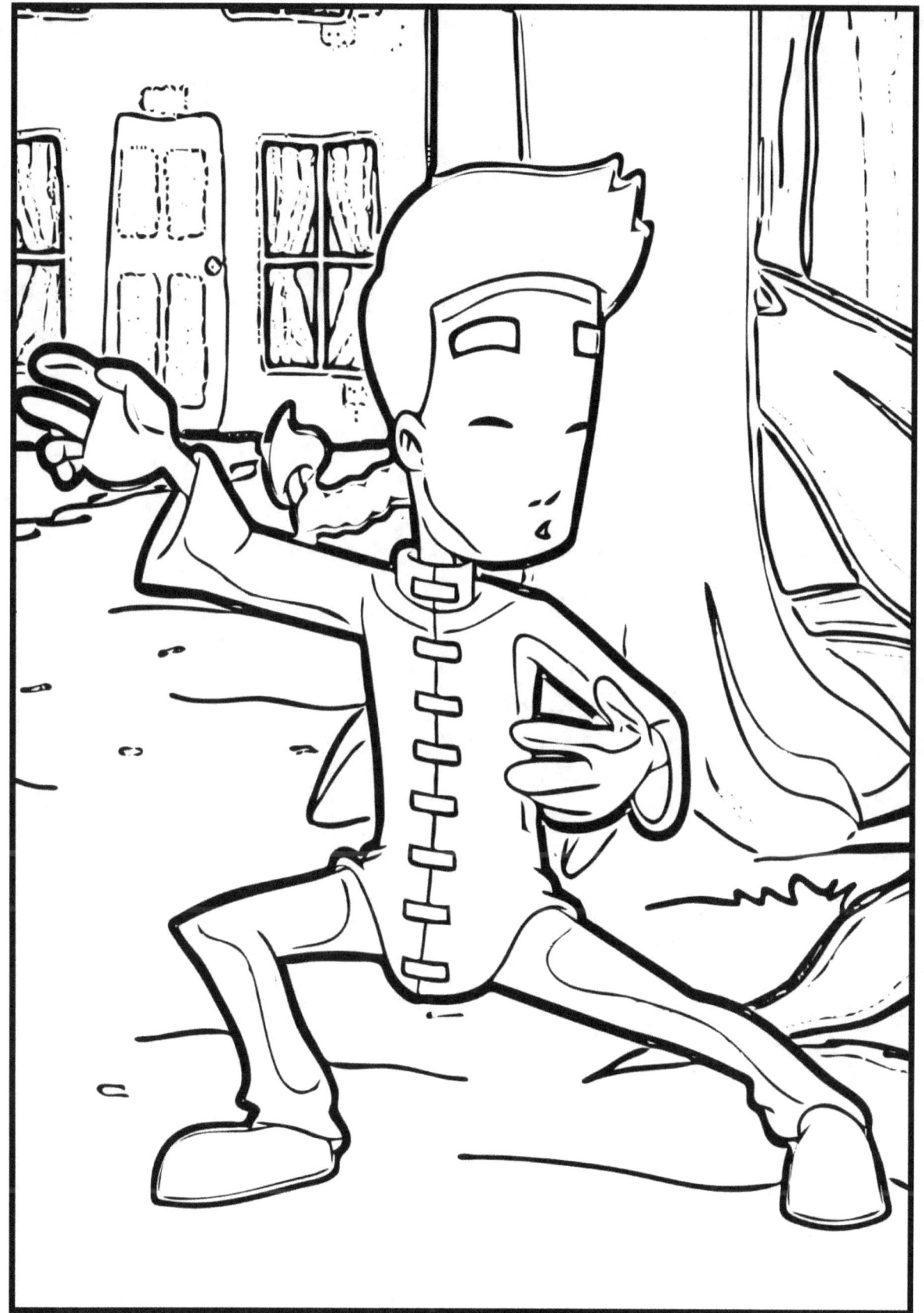

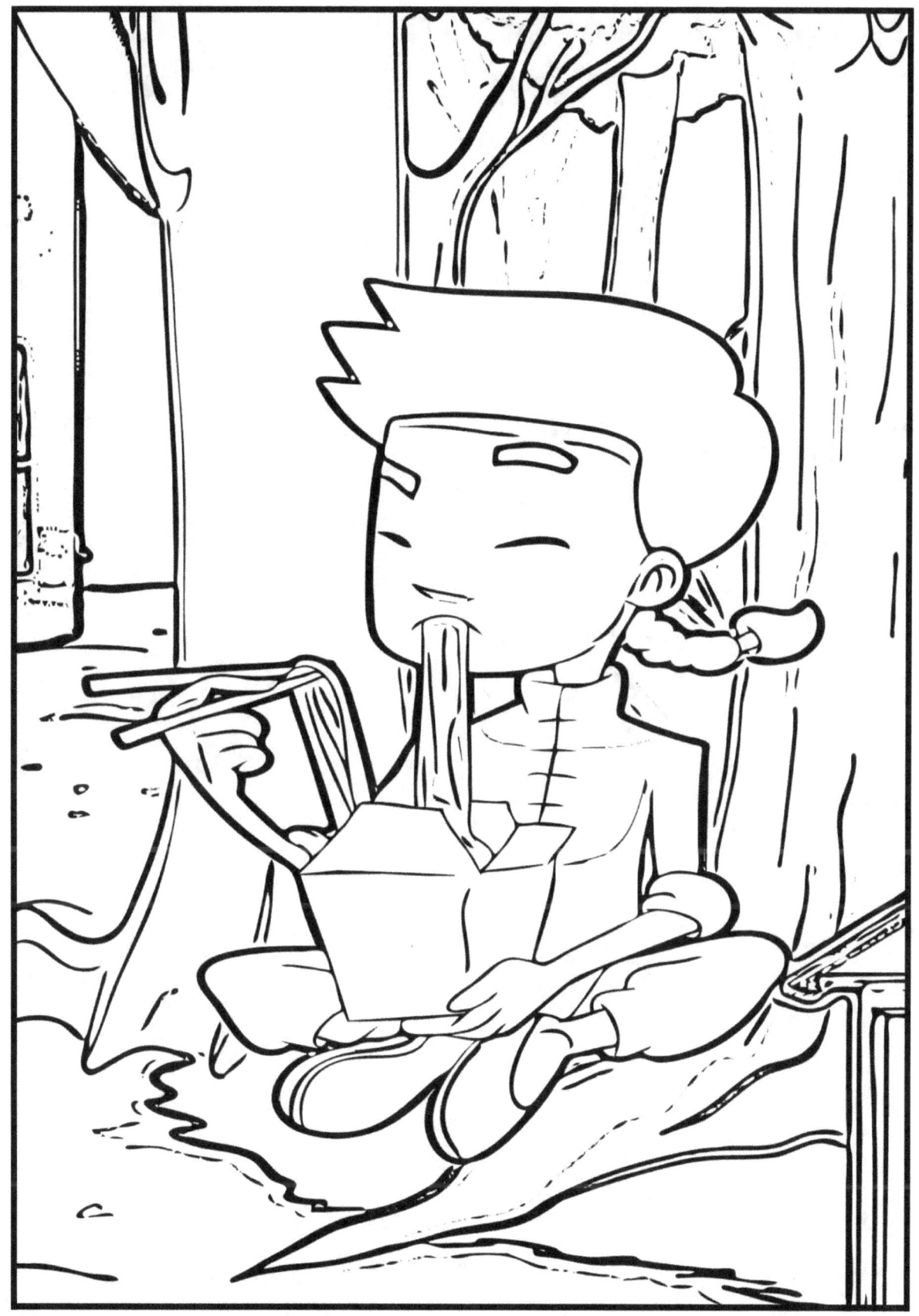

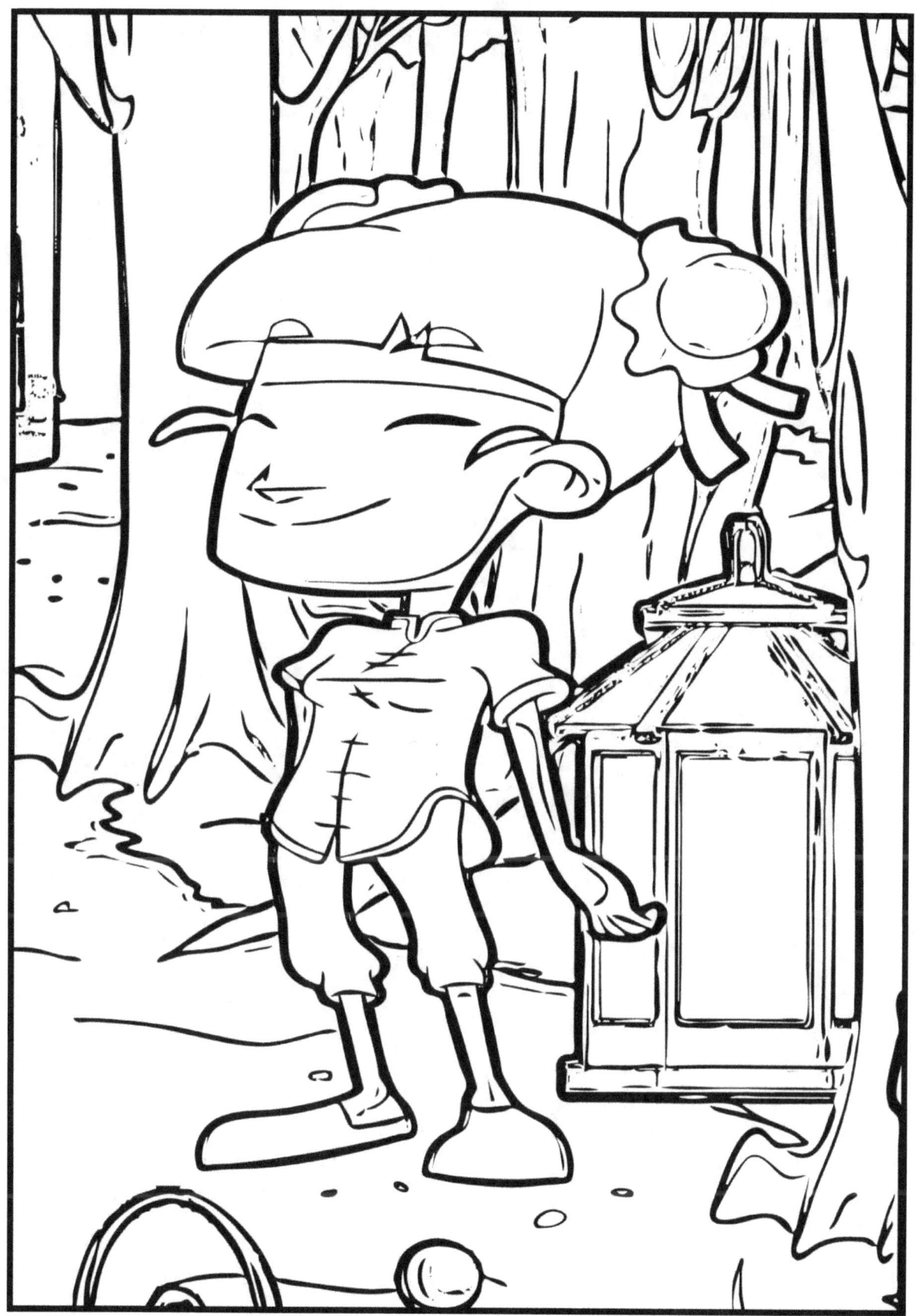

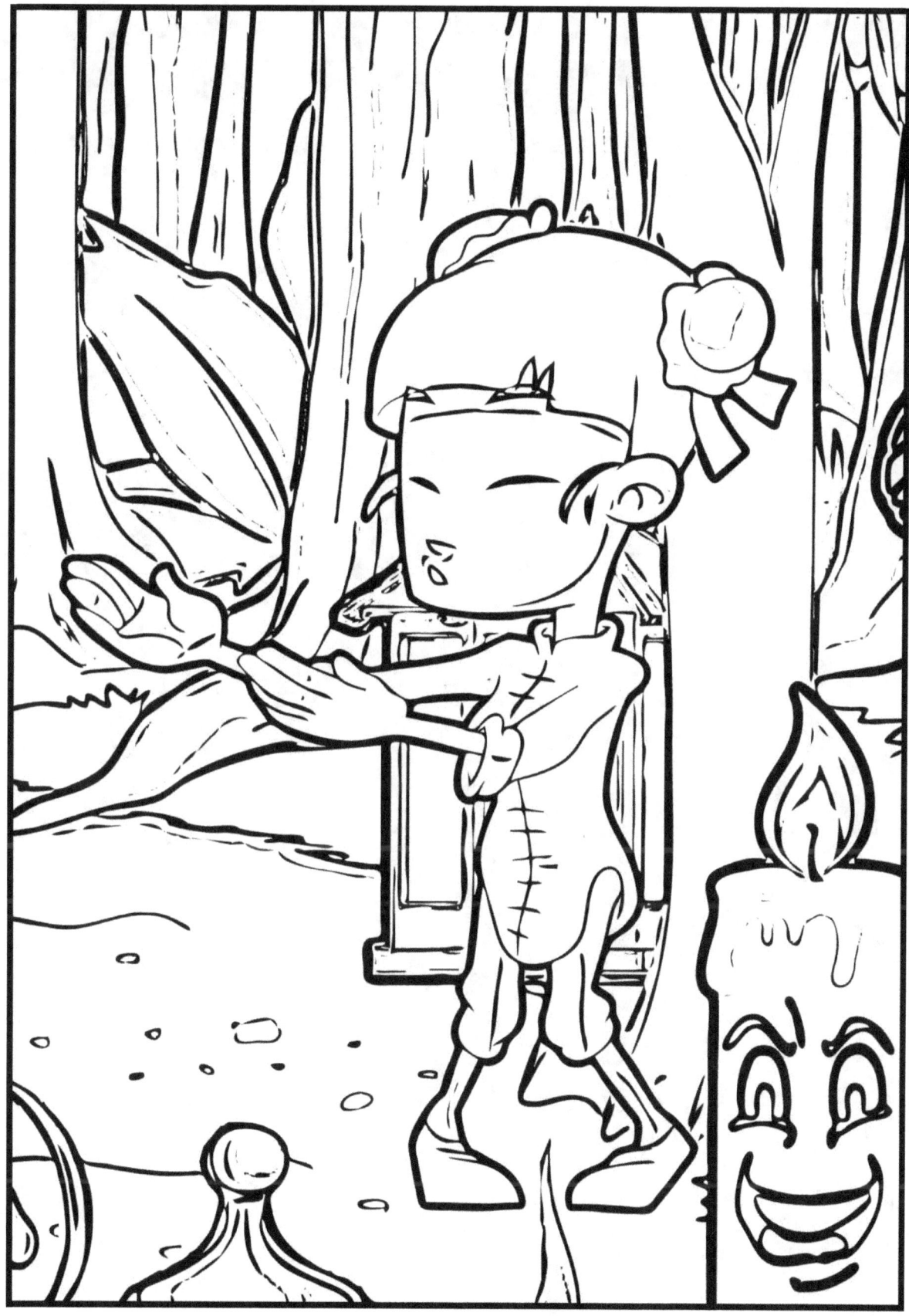

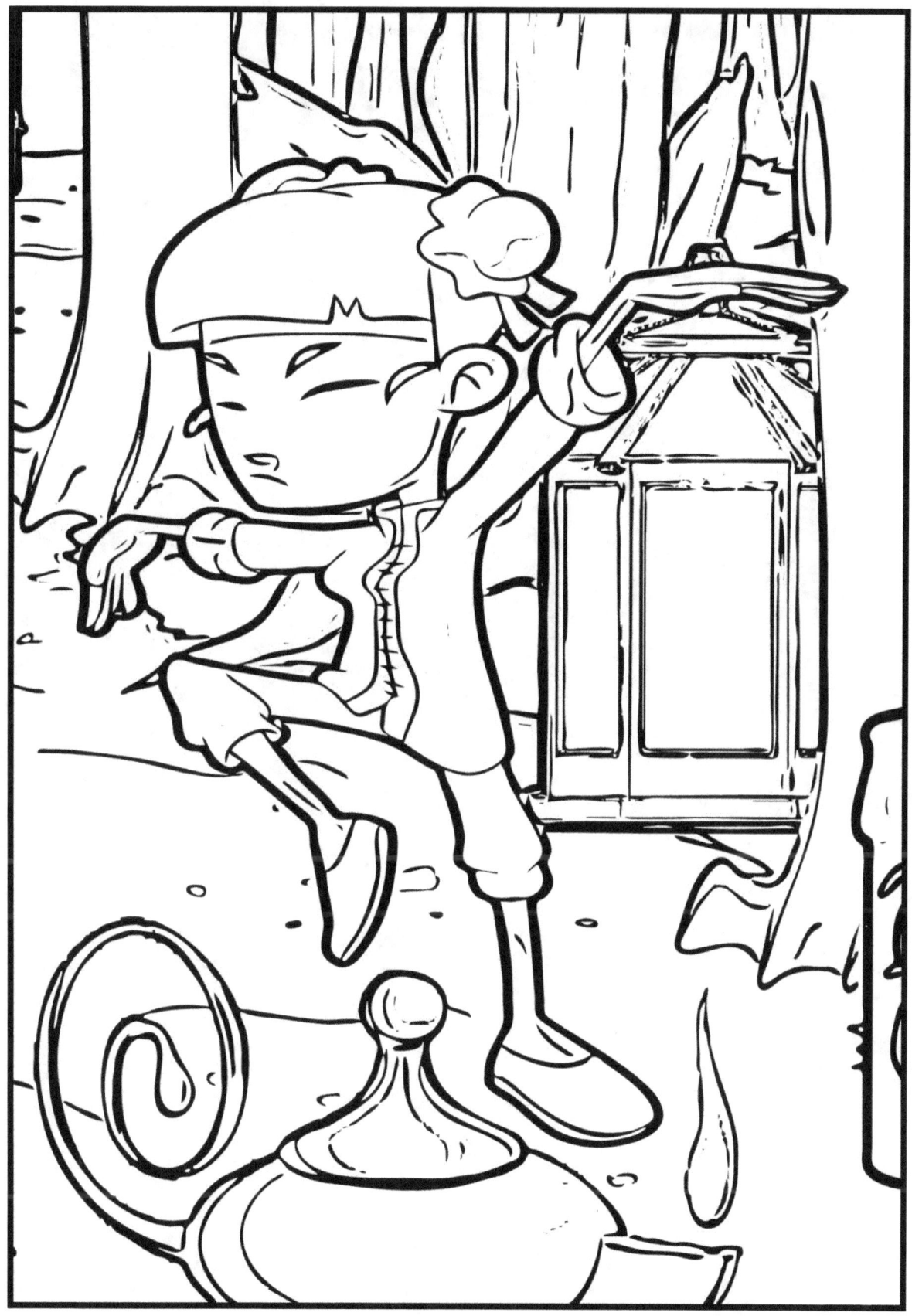

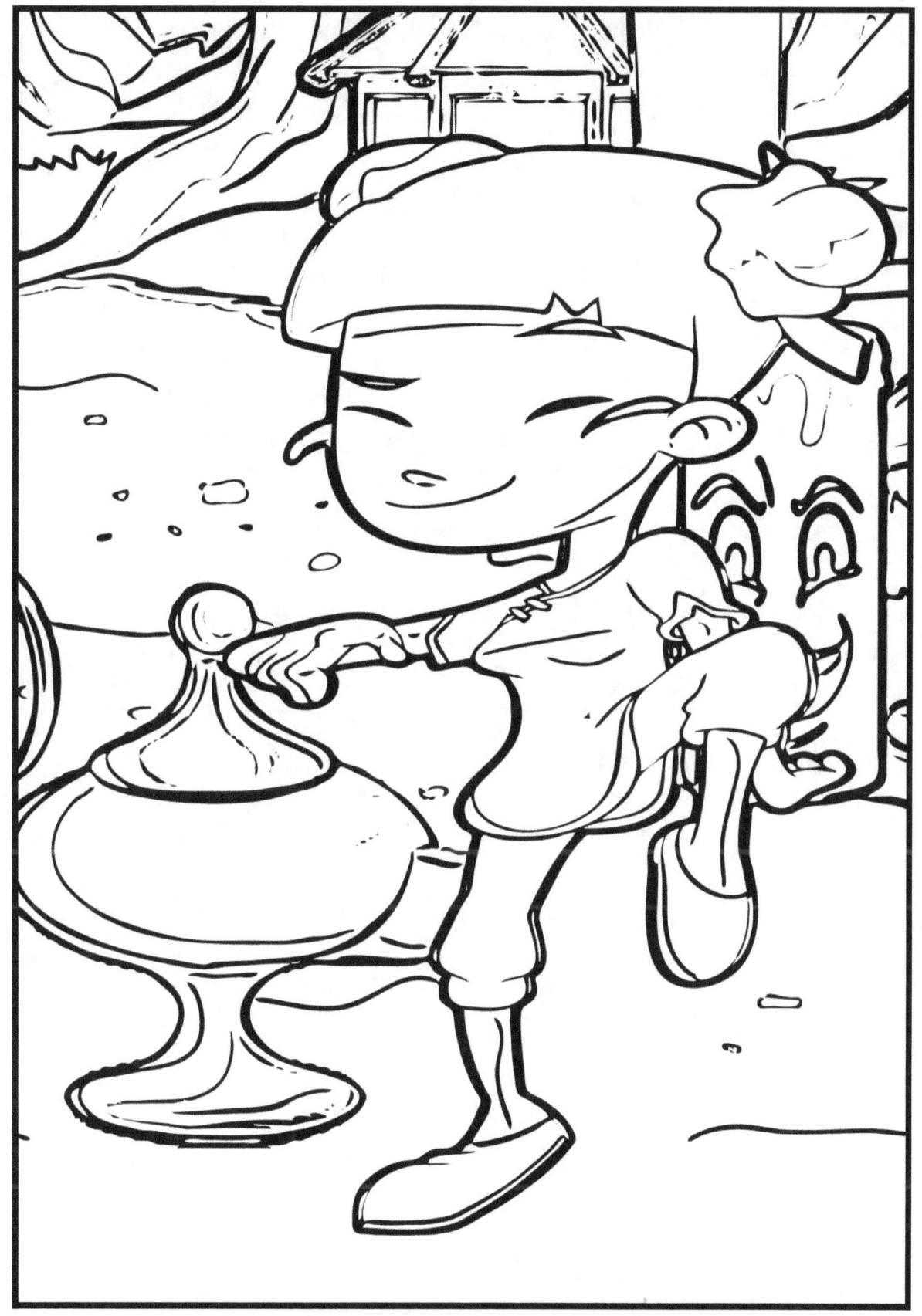

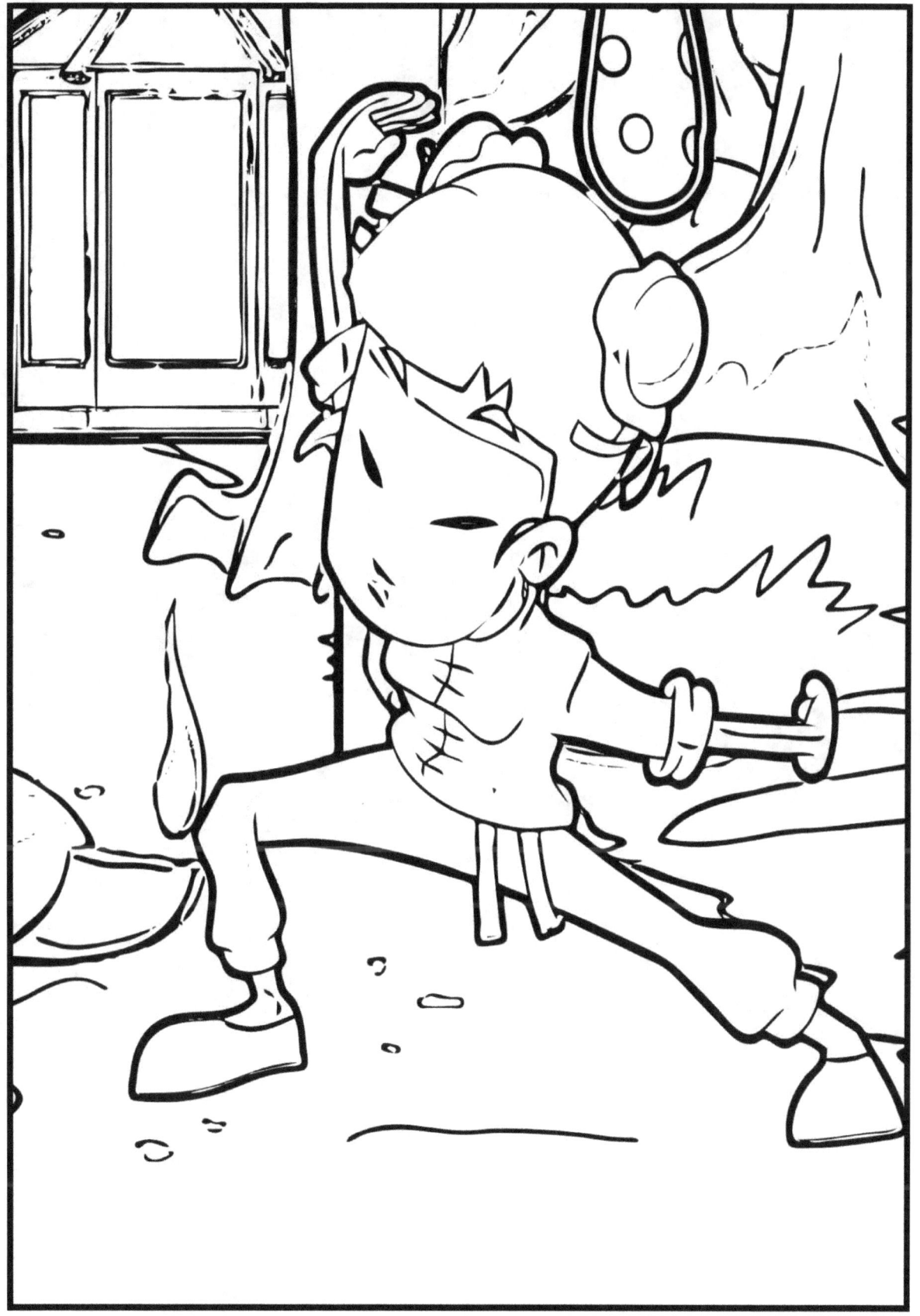

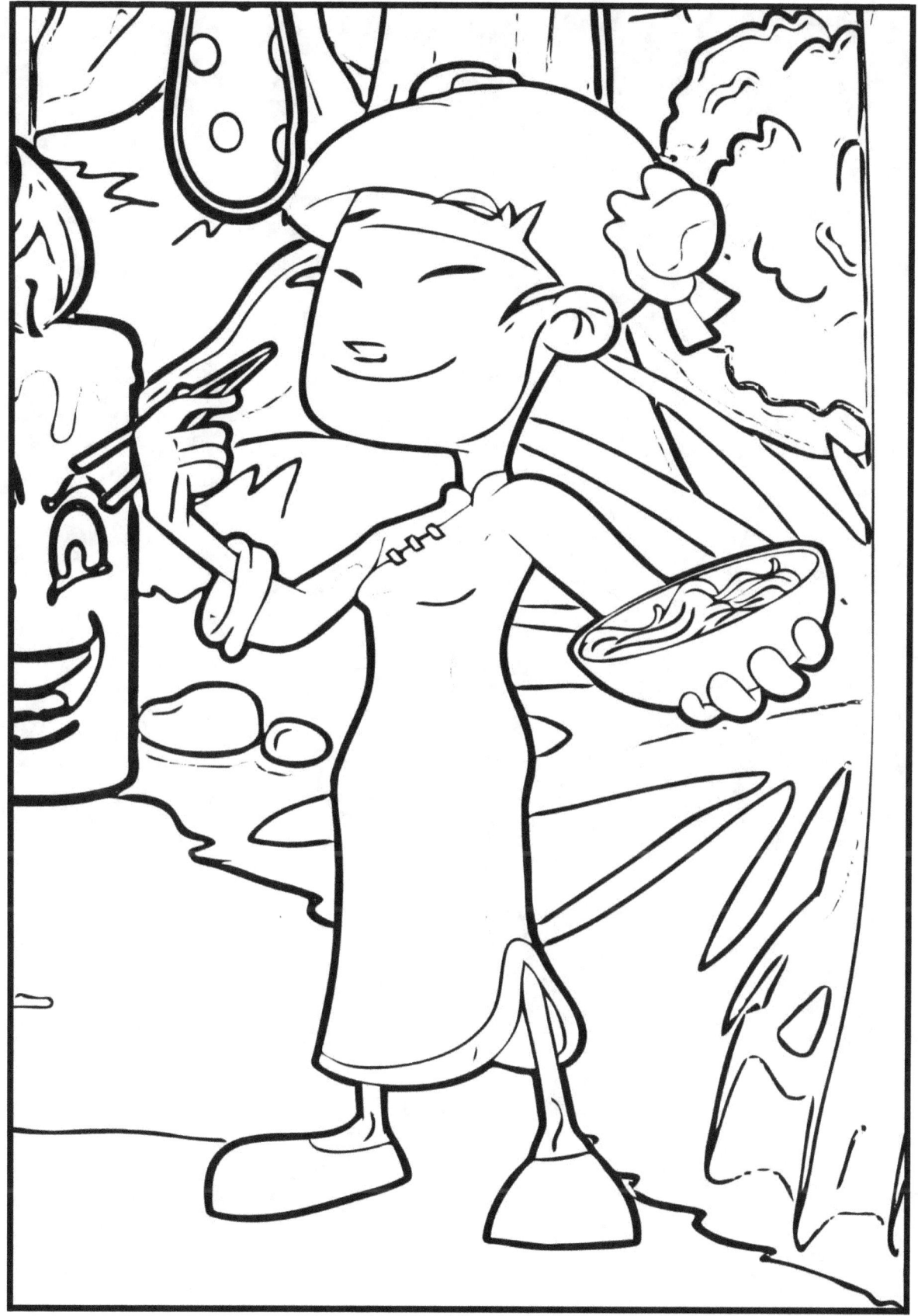

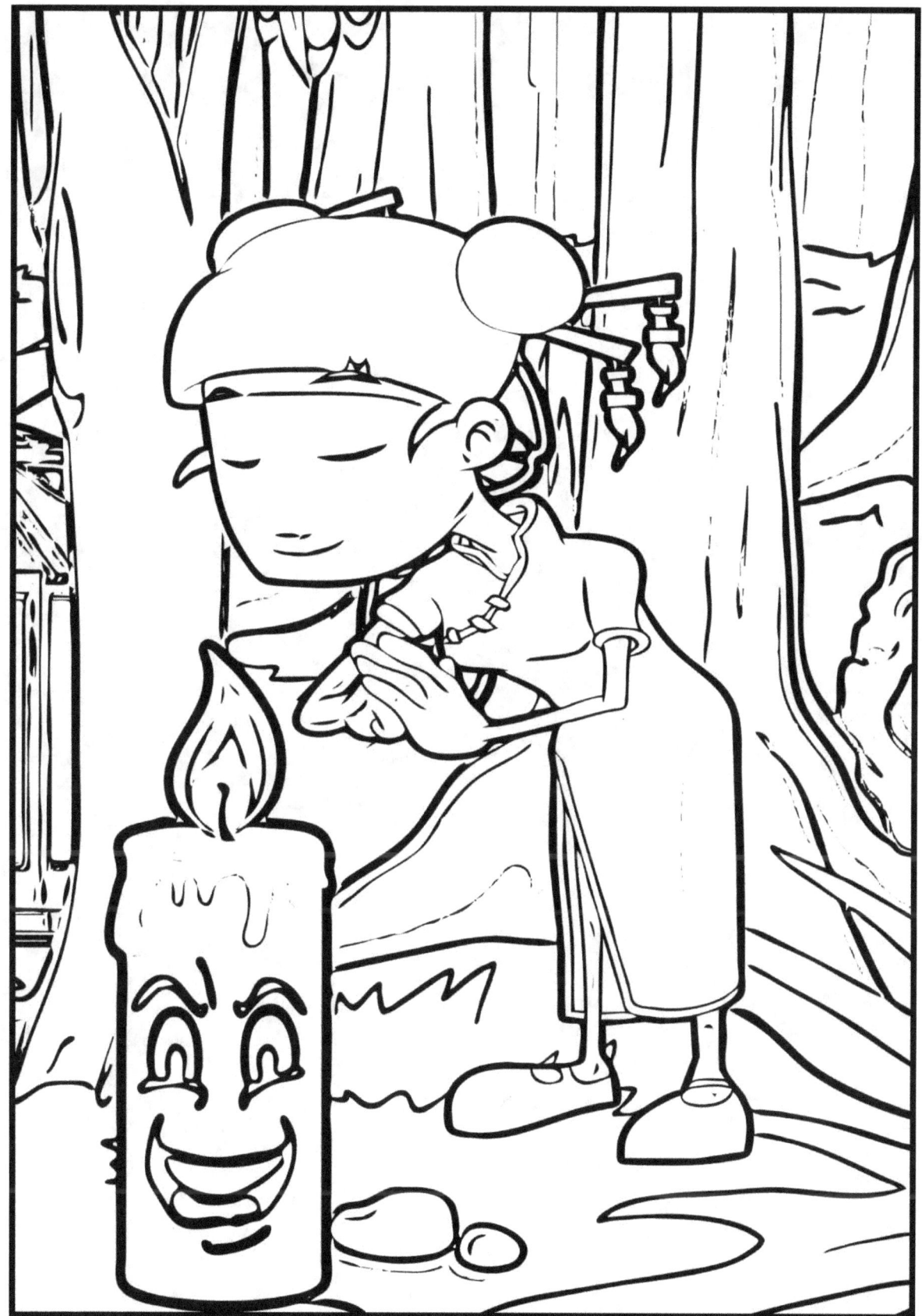

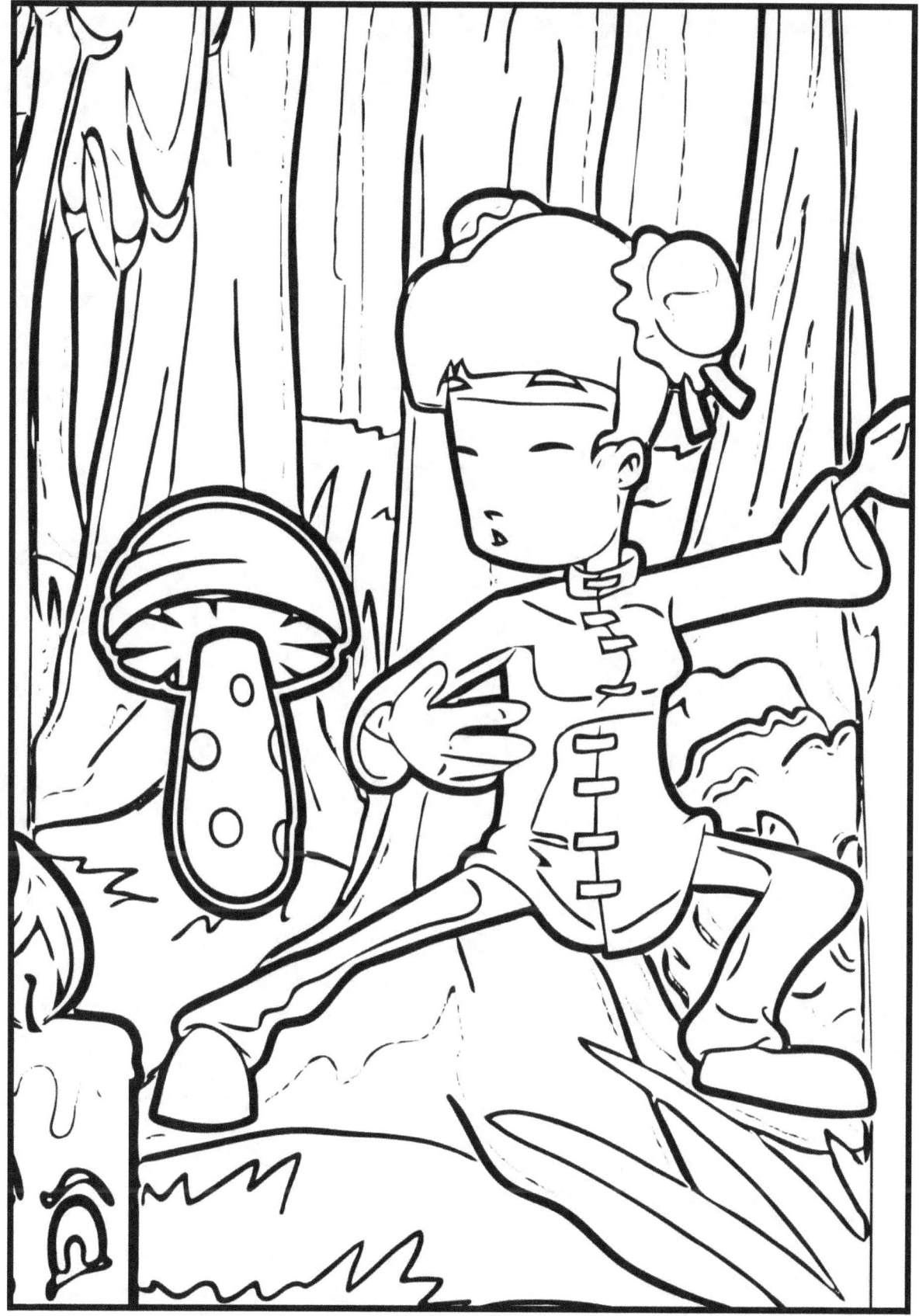

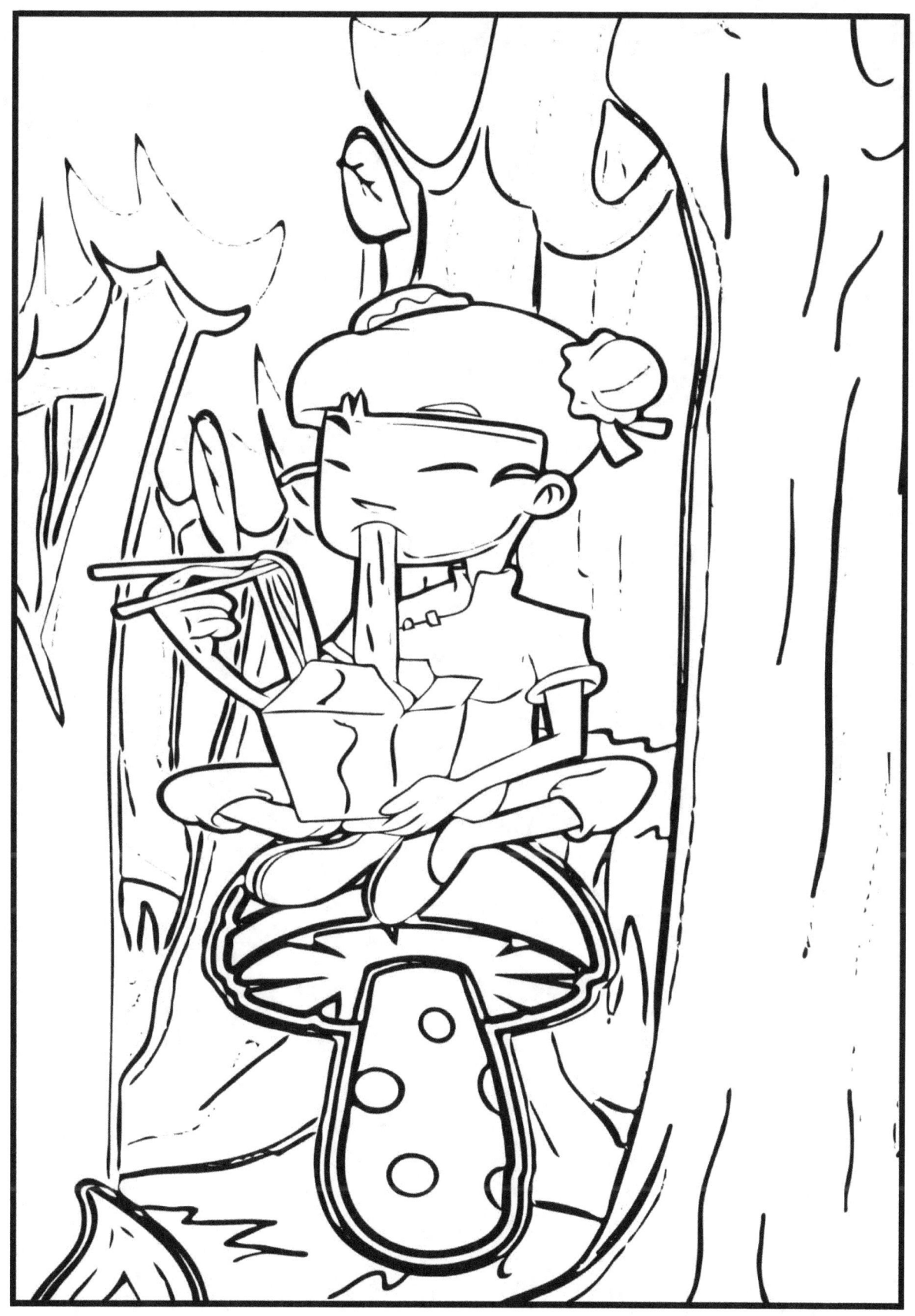

FASHION VICTIM STREET
Coloring Book

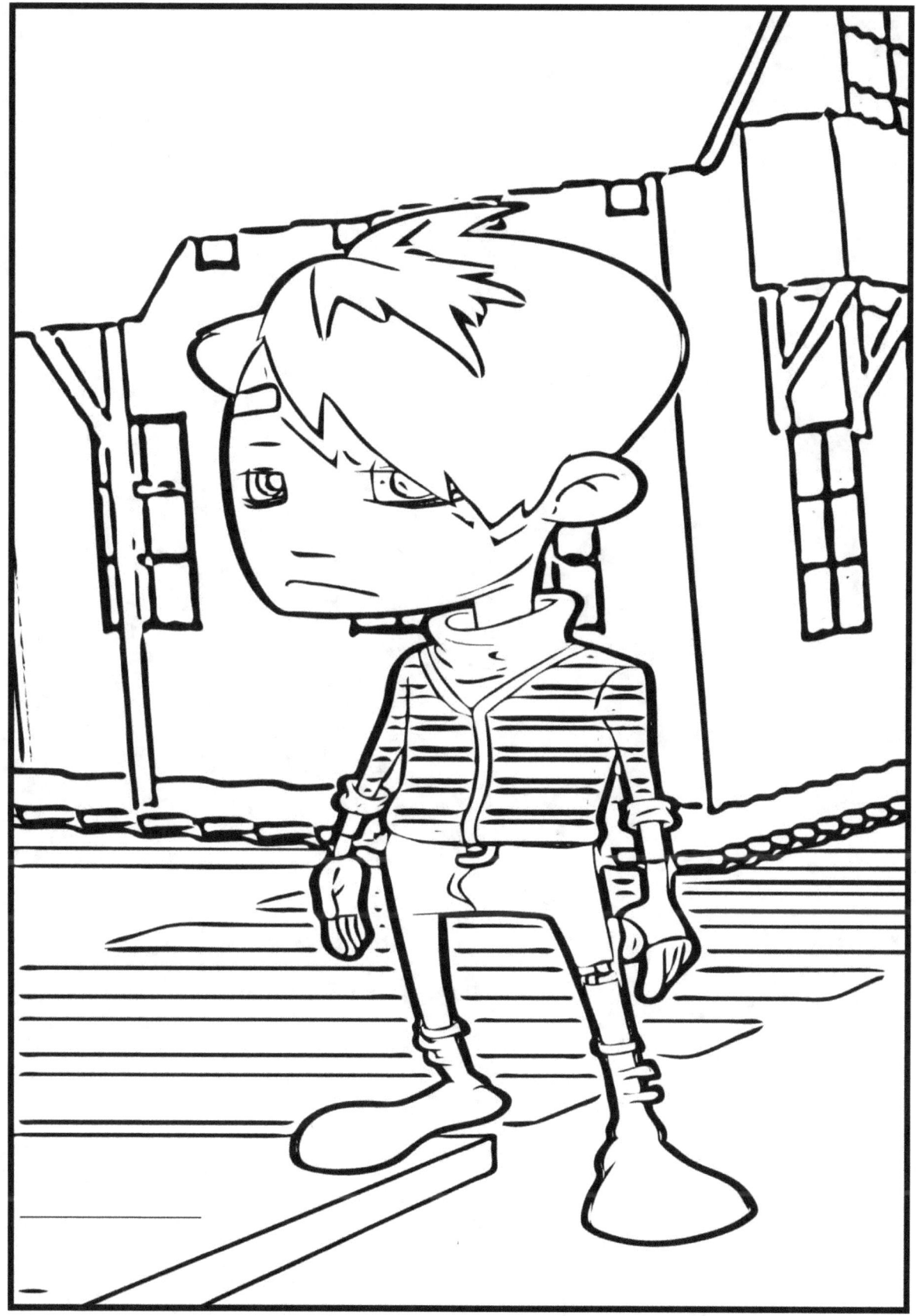

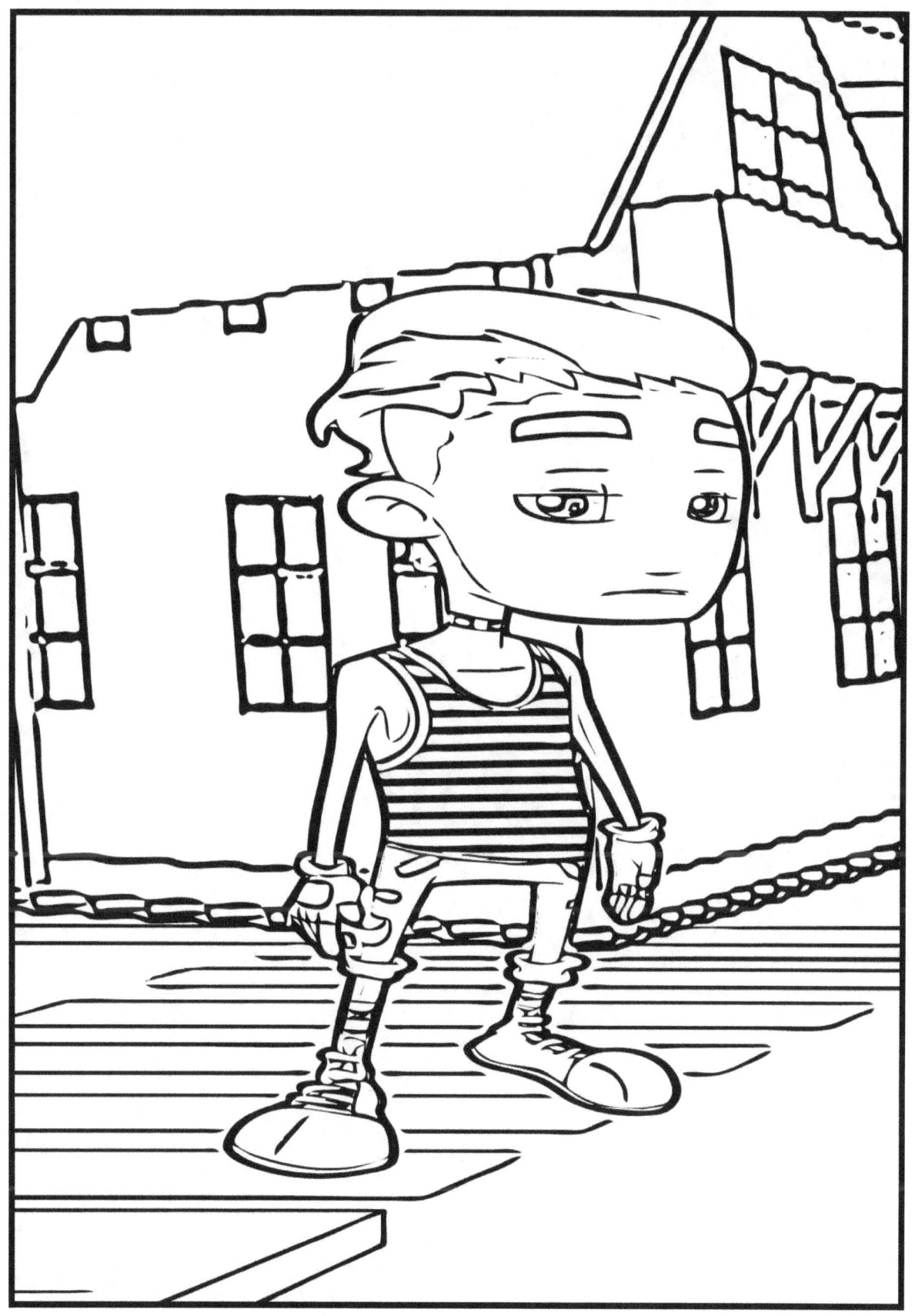

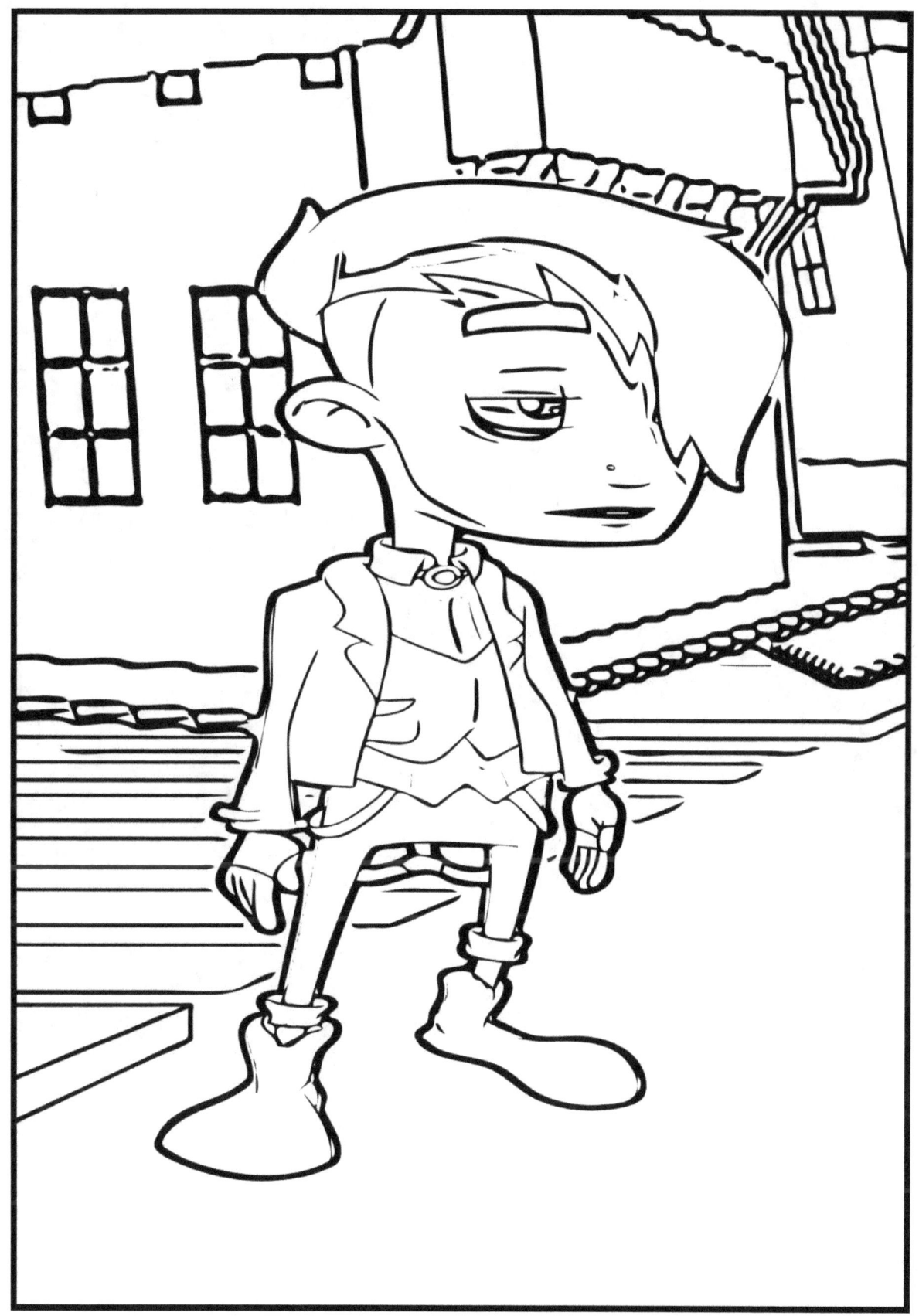

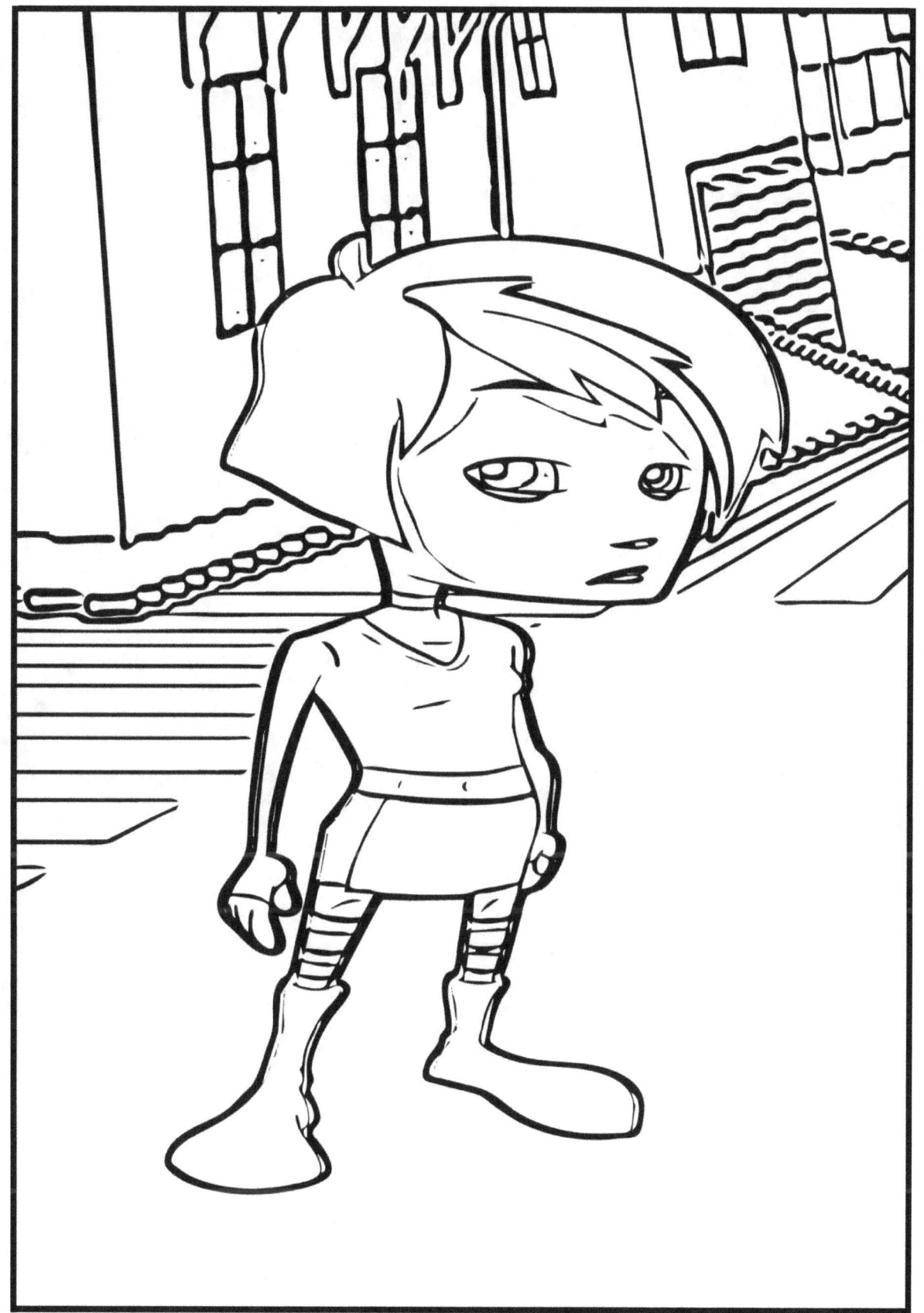

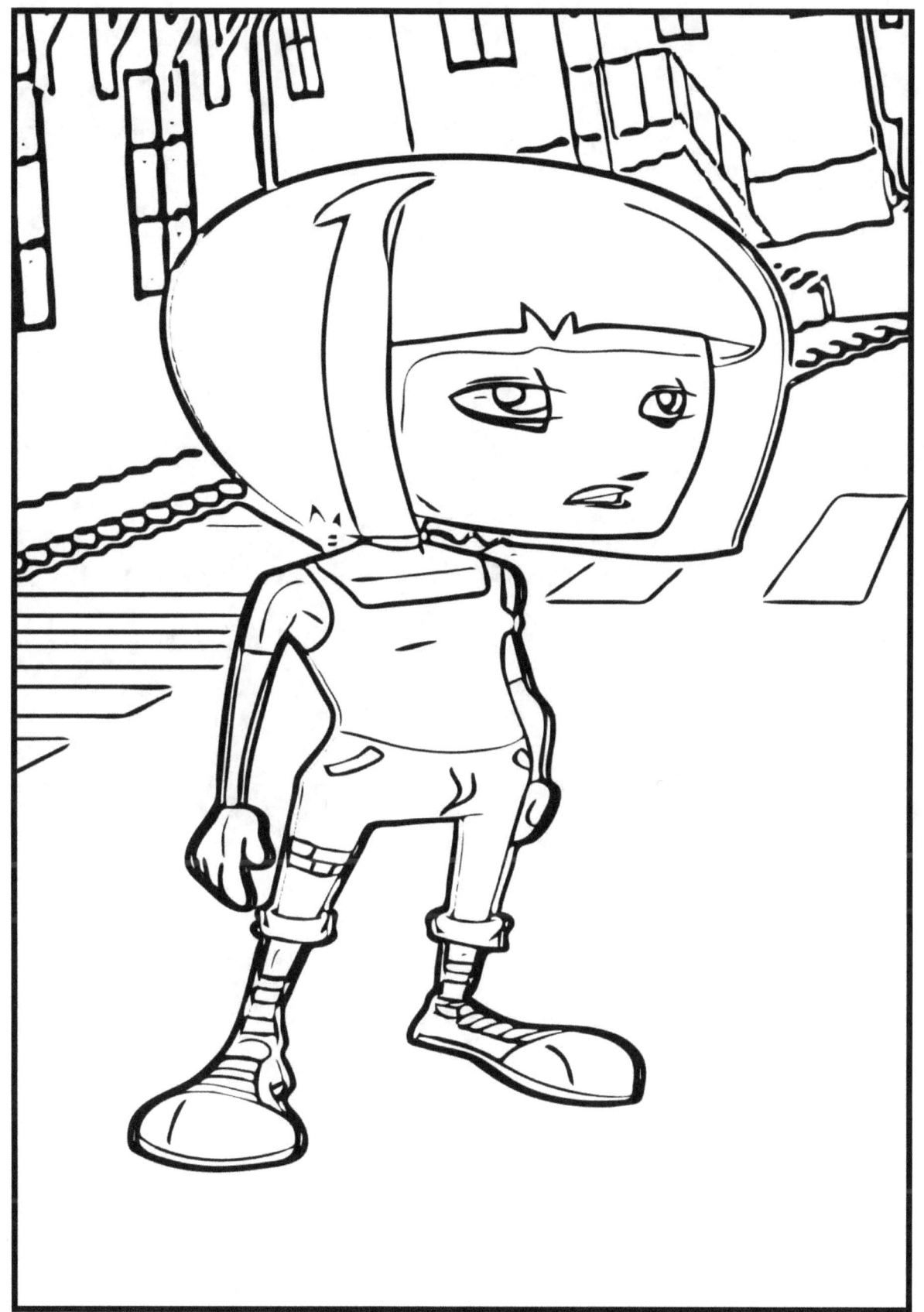

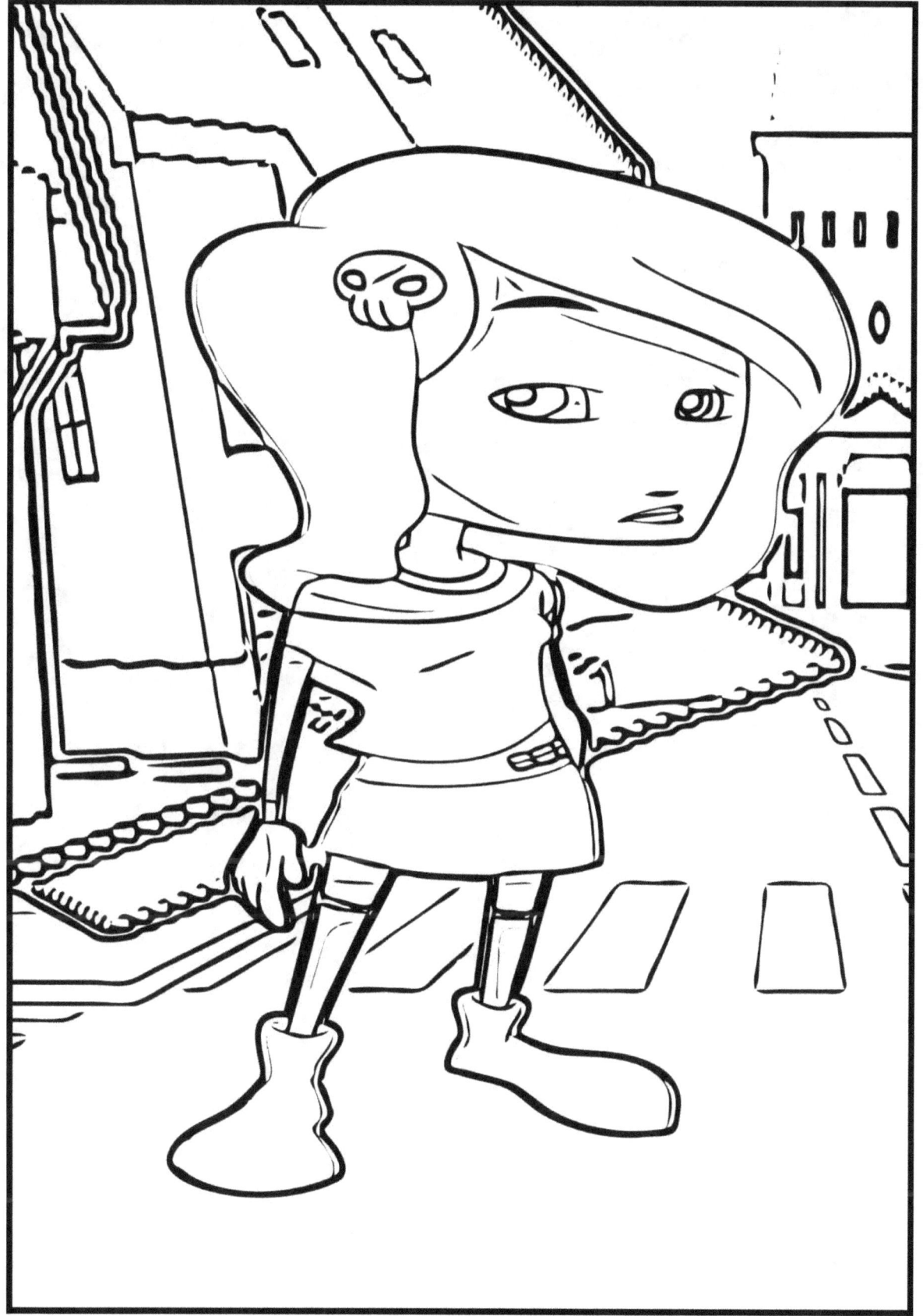

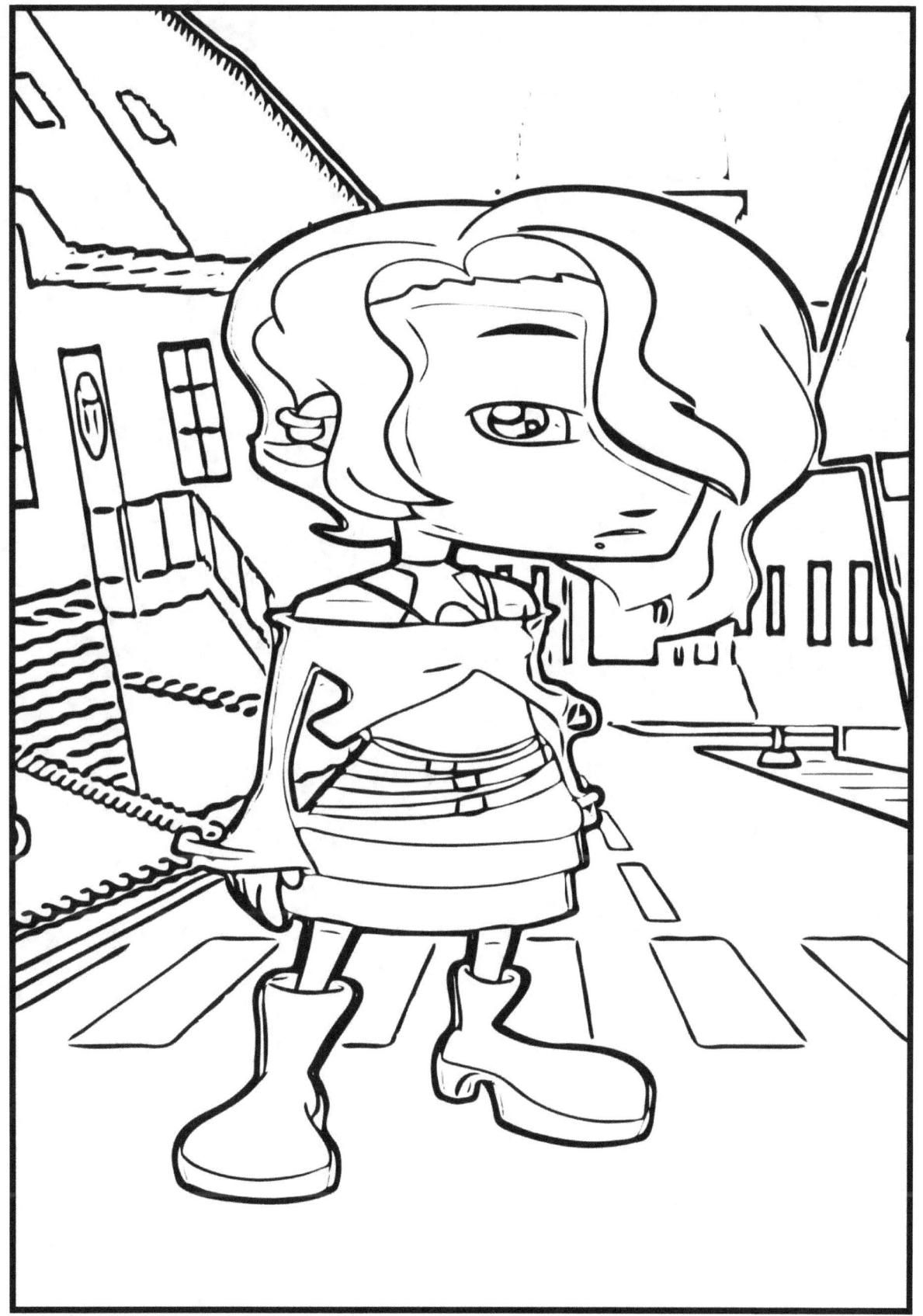

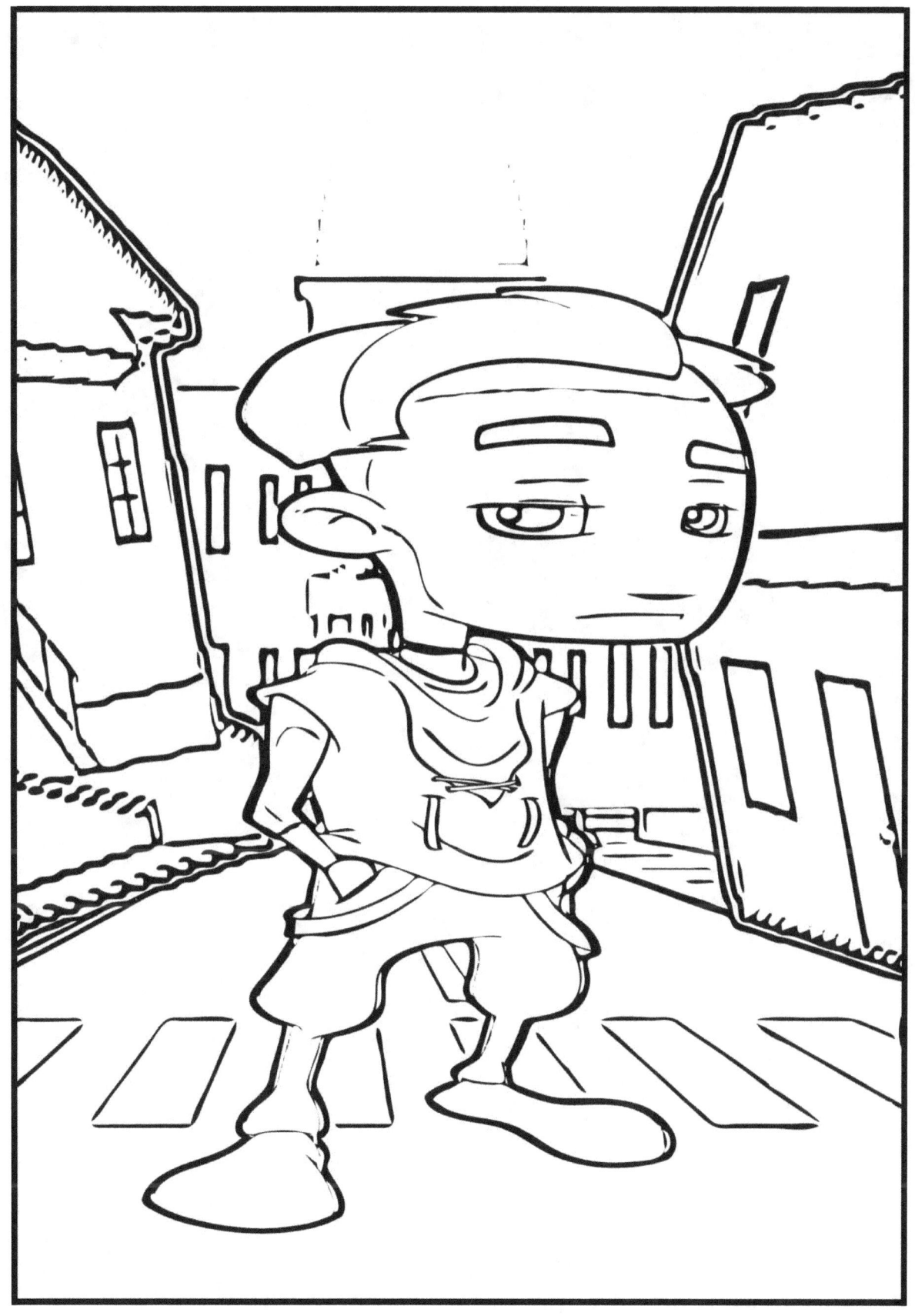

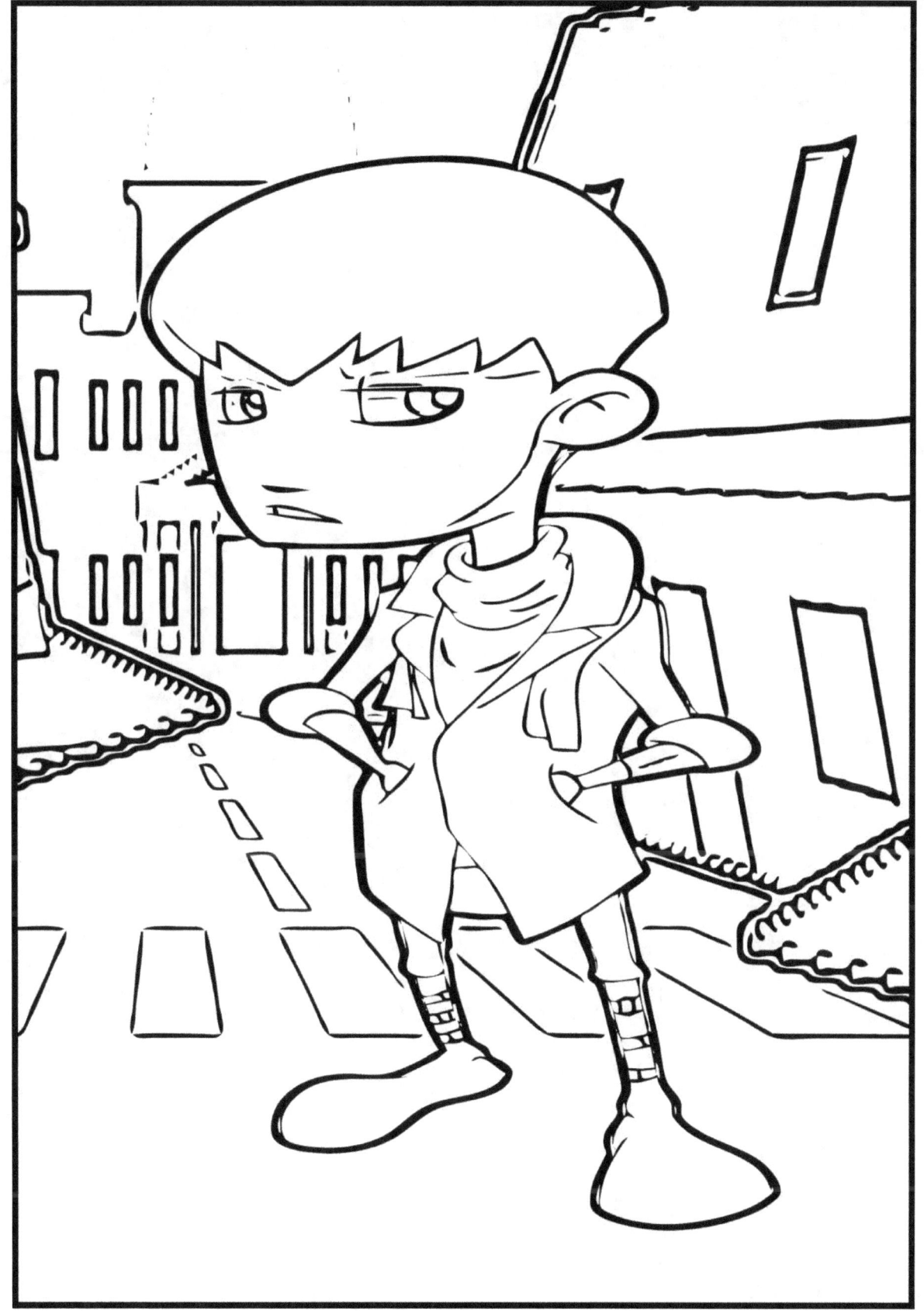

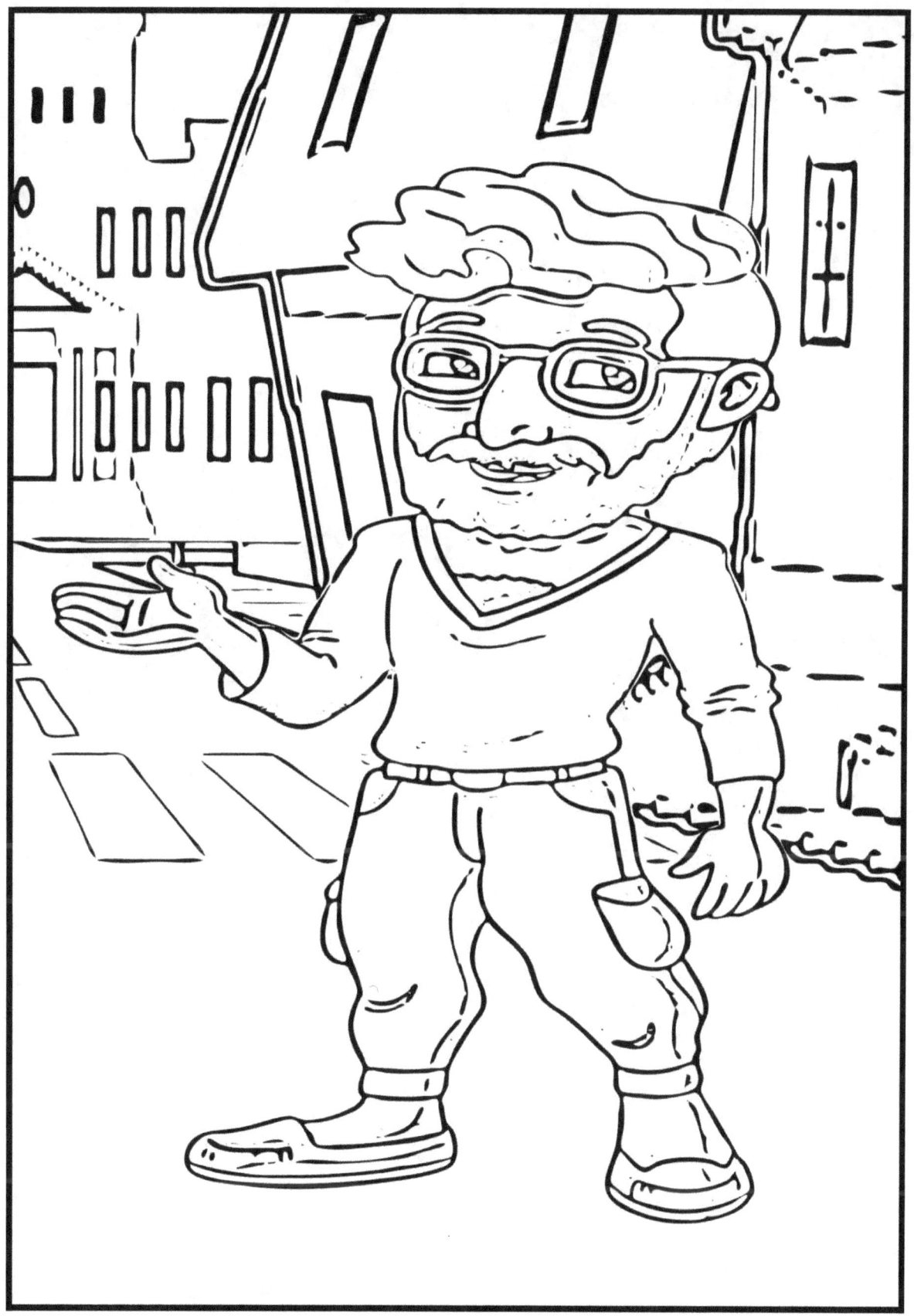

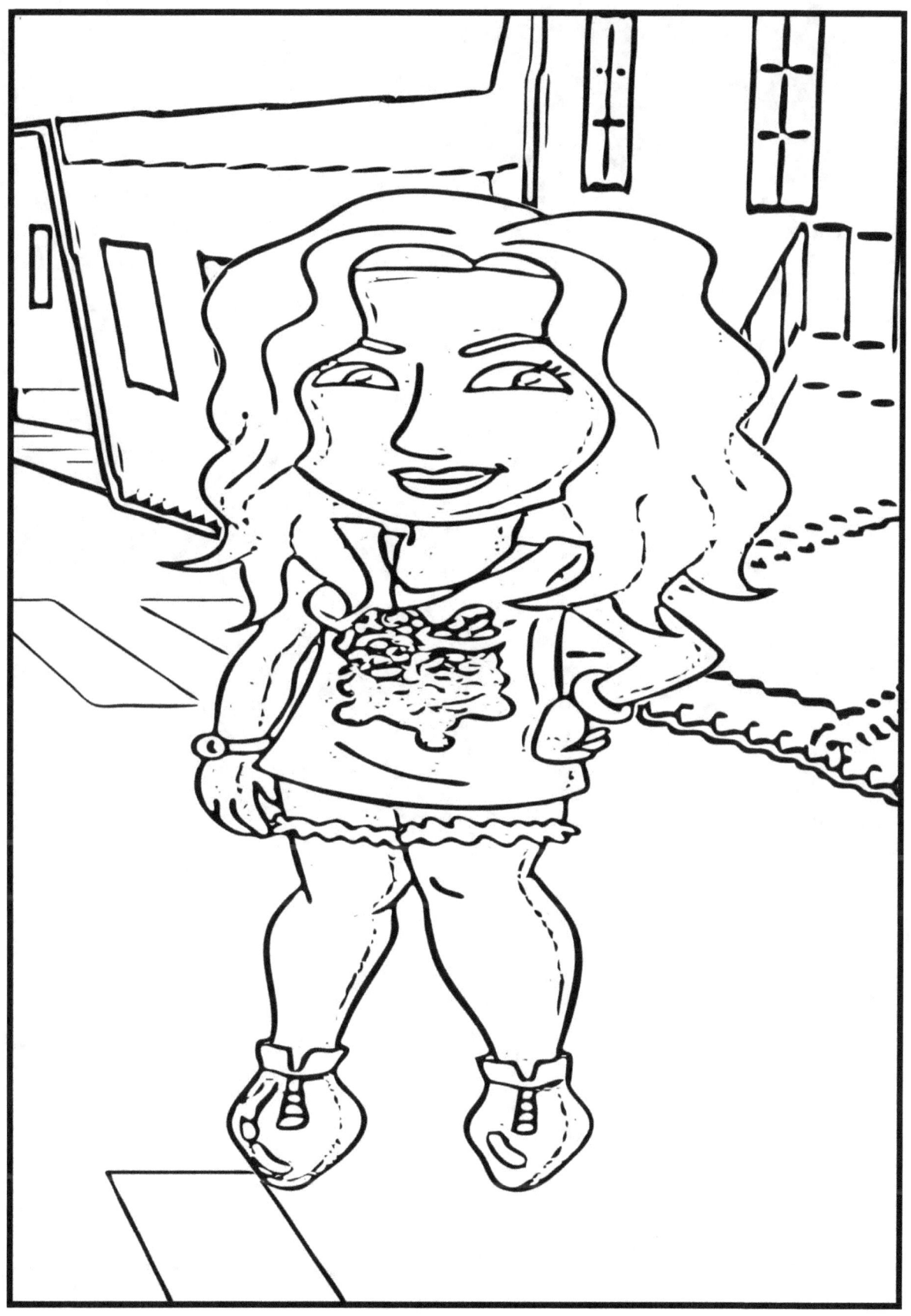

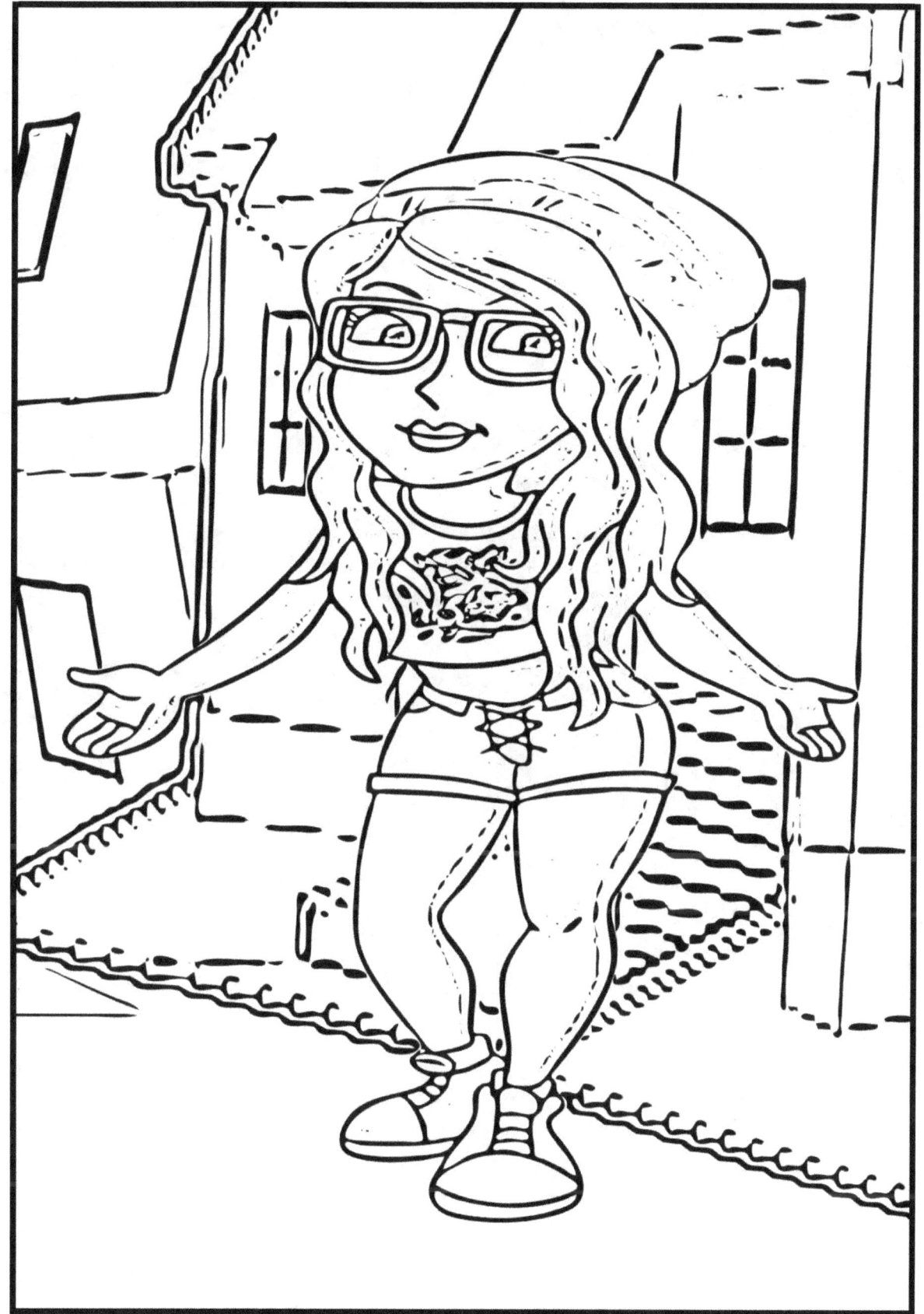

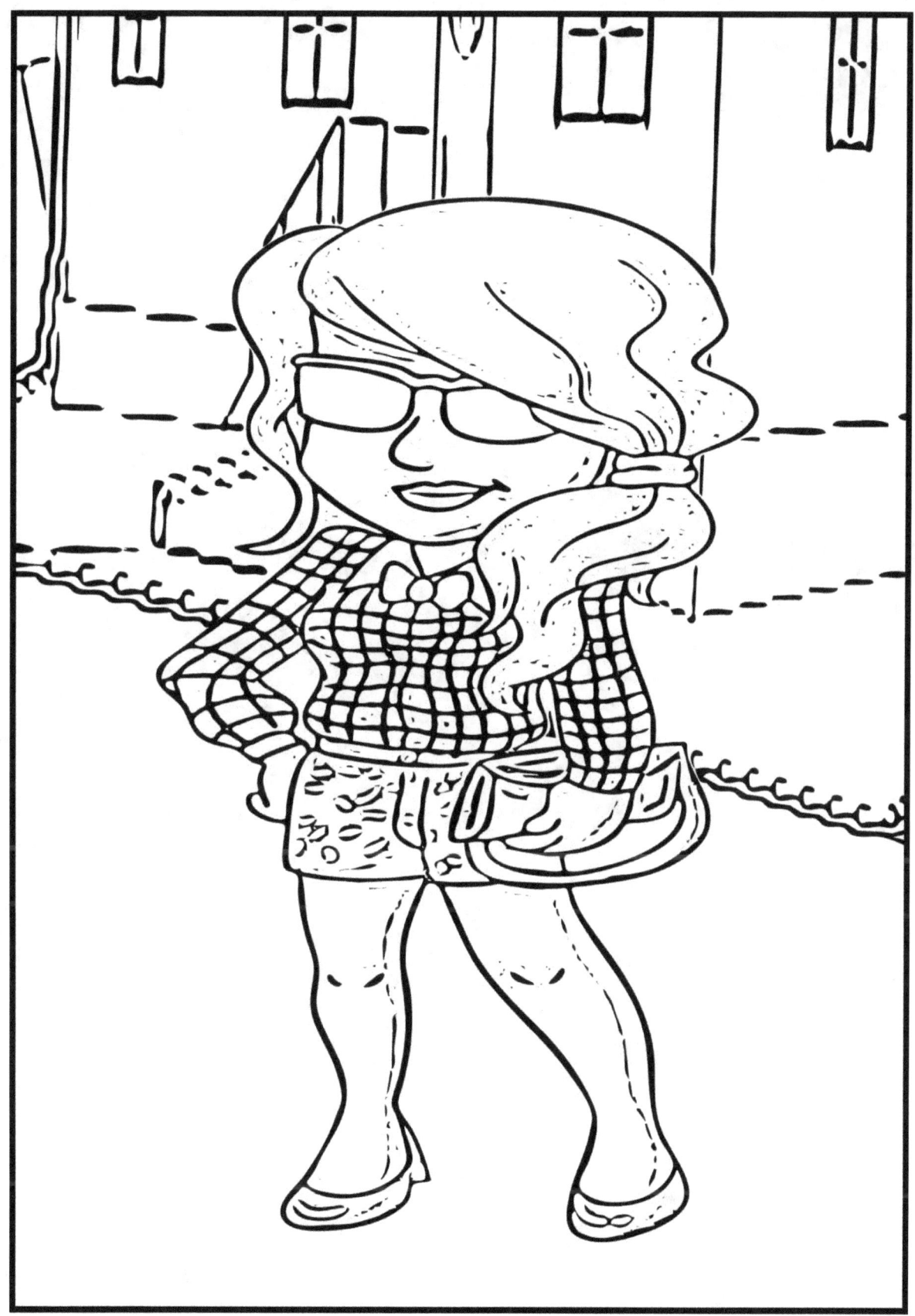

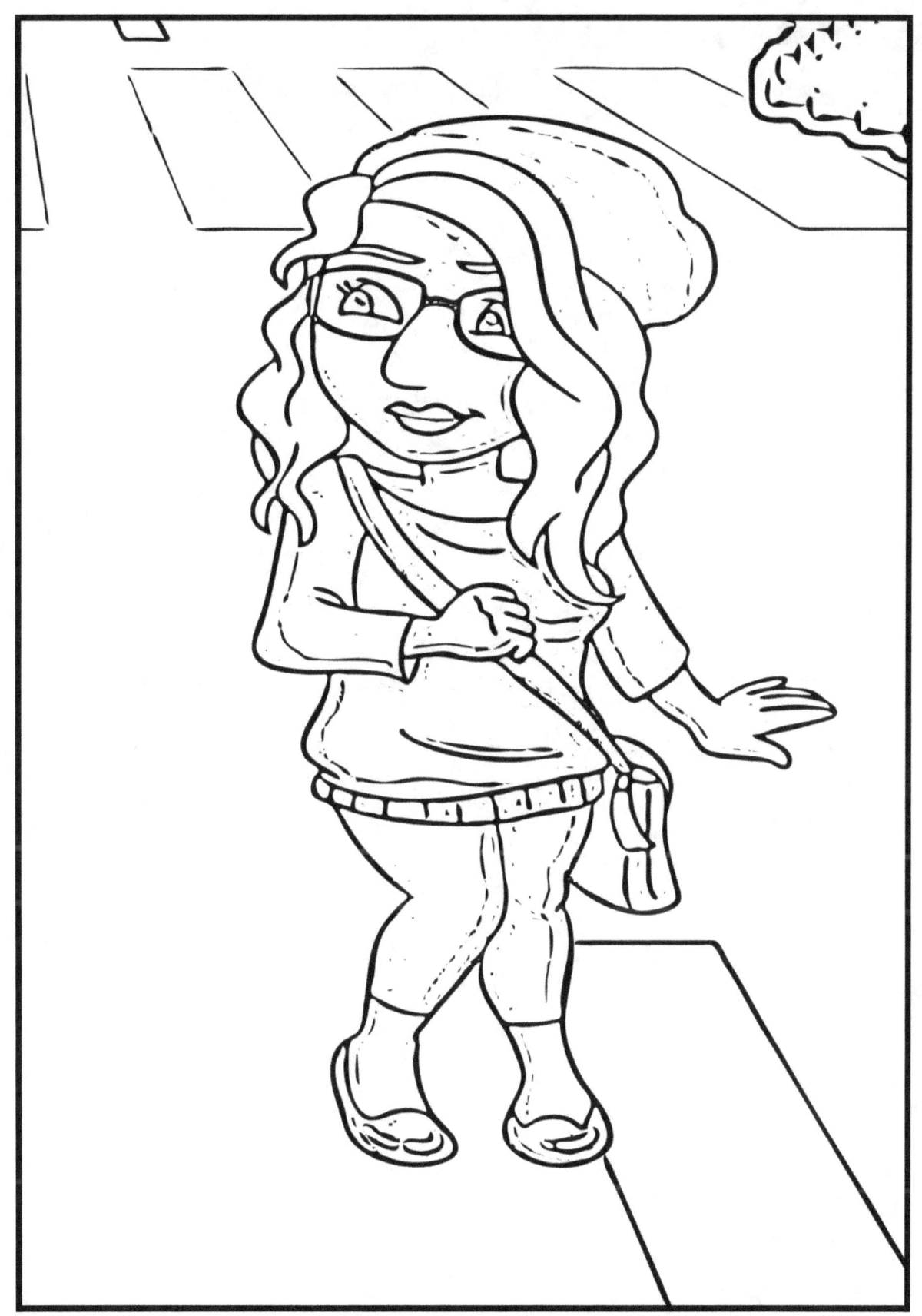

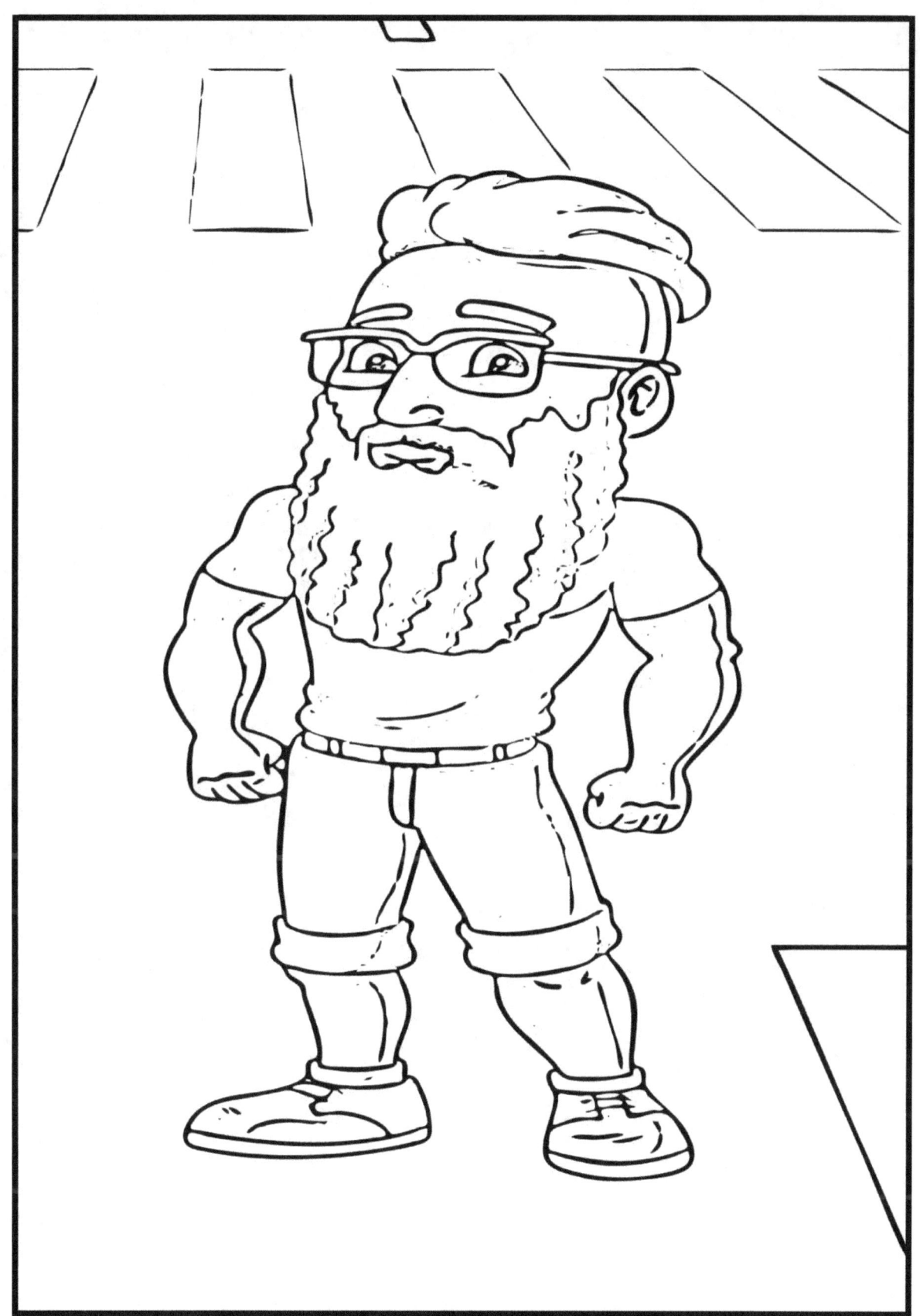

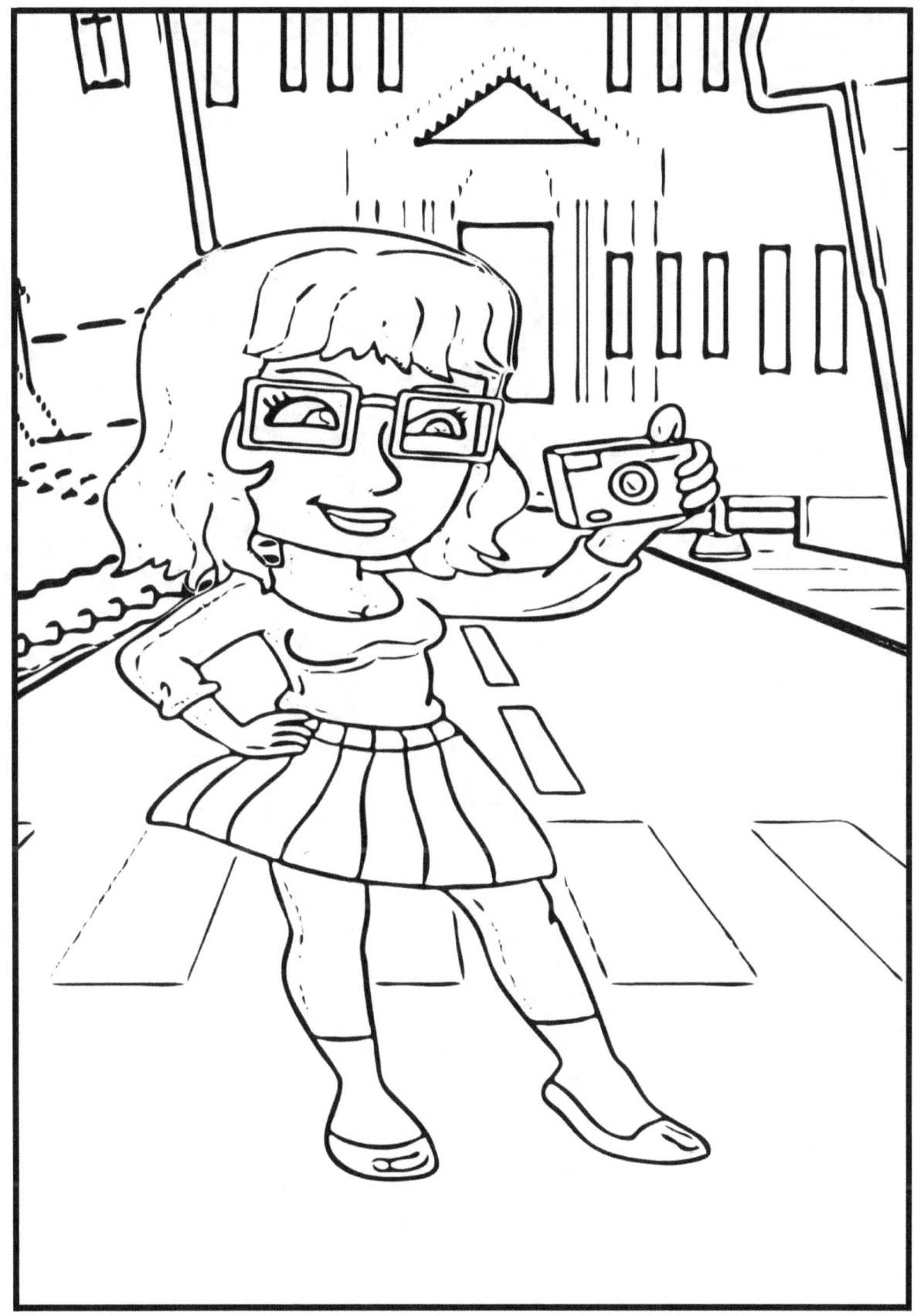

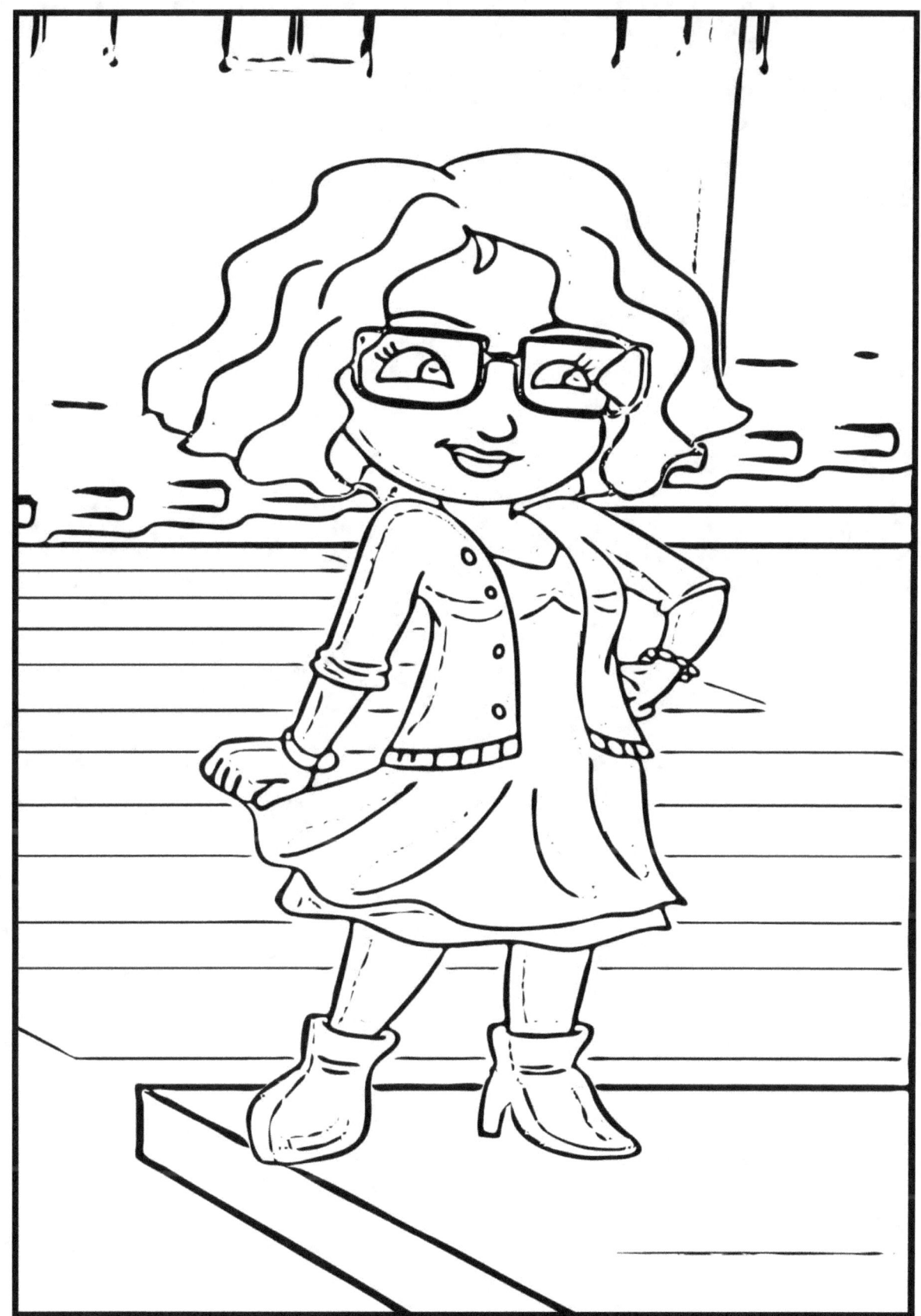

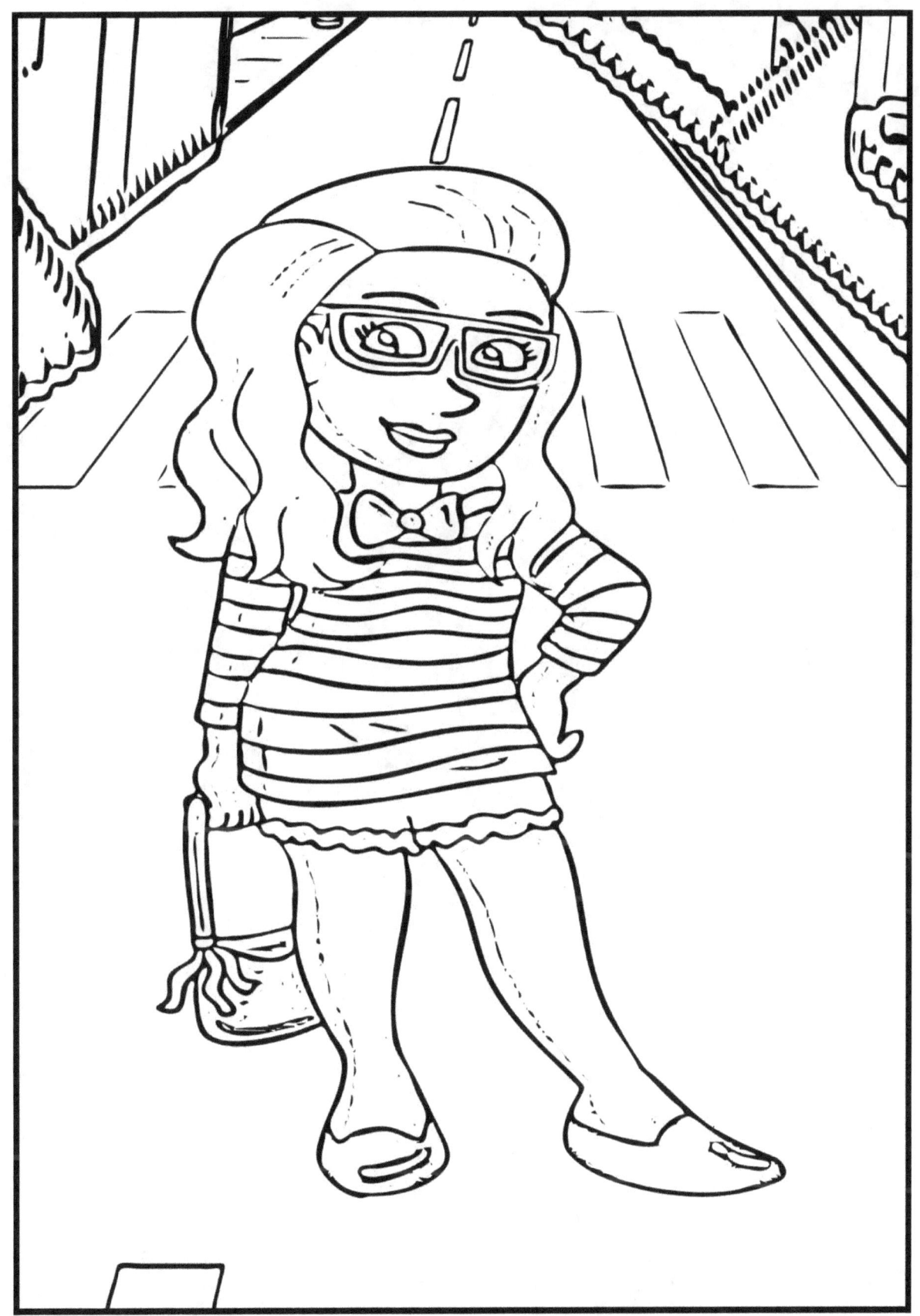